FROLIC

Adventures of a Nudist in Training

MATTHEW FRANKLIN SIAS

PRESS

PRESS

Published by Vulpine Press in the United Kingdom in 2021

Cover by Claire Wood

ISBN: 978-1-83919-154-1

www.vulpine-press.com

This book is dedicated to the memory of Lake Associates Recreation Club and all the fine folks who were members over the years.

Sunday, Naked Sunday

There was something mildly jarring about the sight of an elderly woman gardening in the nude first thing in the morning. Well, it was my morning, anyway, and at 11:18 a.m. the mercury was just climbing into the upper seventies, as measured by the thermometer stuck to the grimy window of the single-wide I'd been calling home for the past two weeks. It wasn't an unpleasant sight, exactly, it was simply that there was much more bobbing and jiggling visible than there would be if the old woman was swathed in fabric. My eyes adjusted to the glaring sun just as I gradually adjusted to the unusual sight in front of me.

The old woman, Dolores, I think her name was, placed her tulips into the window box outside her trailer as gently as if they were newborn babies. Her arthritic hands gathered soil around the roots as she hummed to herself. She stood back looking pleased with her project, and then looked around for a second for a place to wipe her dirty hands. She chose as a towel her ample breasts, as the woman wore nothing but a broad-brimmed sun hat and a pair of green plastic clogs.

As Dolores added more soil to her planting bed, I added a little more Baileys to my coffee and wandered onto the narrow deck that abutted the trailer home. I plopped myself down in one of

1

Grandma's cracked and rickety plastic chairs that were so ubiquitous here at the park. I glanced down at my own attire. While Dolores wasn't ready for the catwalk, I wasn't much of a fashion icon myself. I wore a pair of worn-down moccasins, threadbare socks, green pajama bottoms circa 1995, and a college sweatshirt from a school I never actually attended.

Dolores spotted me, or perhaps just heard the creaking as I had sat down in the rickety chair. She smiled and waved a cheery little salutation, gardening gloves in hand. "Beautiful day!" she said. It was a standard greeting here at Deep Valley Family Nudist Park, or any other nudist park, for that matter.

I waved back. "Morning."

A mower started up a few trailers down and soon the musty odor of cut grass came wafting my way. It was a comforting smell that reminded me of lazy weekends at home in California so many years past, with windows and doors wide open, a warm breeze renewing the stale indoor air, as I ignored the inevitability of homework and chores. The acrid odor of a charcoal barbecue wafted from a lot nearby.

Sundays were lazy for some here at Deep Valley, but for others they were an opportunity for lot maintenance: weeding, watering plants, and—God help us—weed whacking. I cringed as I recalled the man I had seen last week, wearing a visor, safety glasses, battered tennis shoes, and nothing else, in full attack mode against the green blades of fescue that threatened to engulf his carrots and radishes. At least his face and feet would be protected, but God forbid he should nick his tallywhacker with a weed whacker. That would be an interesting one to explain to the paramedics.

Fifteen days I'd been here, existing in a sort of surreal, sun-drenched limbo at the Deep Valley Family Nudist Park, neither a member nor a visitor—certainly not a nudist. Grandma, my father's eccentric and iconoclastic mother, had been kind enough to let me stay at her home for a while after my untimely departure from my professorial appointment at Western Washington University in Bellingham. One rough week was all it took, and I was suddenly stuck standing in the unemployment line, hat in hand, with all the rest of the schmucks. Thirty-four years old with a Ph.D. in Biology and I was back to square one. I may as well be living in my parents' basement, playing World of Warcraft deep into the night, eating Cheetos and becoming walrus sized.

I was a solid professor, though, or so I thought. I was, perhaps, a bit dull, but I knew my subject forwards and backwards, inside and out, down to the atomic level, stayed hours after lectures to answer students' questions, and my exams were wickedly tough and in essay form. My final examinations lasted up to eight hours and were endurance contests of the brain. I basically lived at the university, keeping a bunk and pillow beside my desk, and would often spend three days at a time there without going home.

Admittedly, however, I was chronically late to meetings and the rest of the department never seemed to be too amused by the gin on my breath or the bloodshot eyes that belied a reliance on ethanol that was increasing with every passing semester. It was true that I had a drinking problem, but I functioned reasonably well despite being half-stewed the majority of the time. Was I an alcoholic? It was a question I had mulled in my brain ad nauseam before I decided it was all really just a question of semantics. Personally, I preferred the term "alcohol enthusiast" but I always knew deep down I was deflecting the problem with my usual dry and irreverent humor. I'd be lucky if I hadn't pickled myself by the time I was forty.

But be that as it may, I suspected it was going to take me a while to find a new job, and until I had gotten back on my feet, I would be drinking Grandma's gin, brushing up my resume, soaking in the sun, and watching the eclectic mix of naked characters traipse past my window. One could find worse entertainment.

Deep Valley Family Nudist Park, located a mile up a long, winding, pothole-filled, rutty gravel road off Highway 20 in East Skagit County on the western side of Washington State, had been in existence for decades, though its heyday had long since passed. Like nudist clubs all over the nation, their members were aging and dying off, their leadership unable to attract a younger crowd to replace them. Nudists from Bellingham, Snohomish County, Eastern Washington, and as far away as Vancouver, B.C. flocked to the park in droves in the mid-1980s, before the age of the Internet and compulsive electronic self-absorption. There was always a volleyball game or two going on any given sunny weekend, which in the Pacific Northwest meant July 4 to mid-September, before the rains and the darkness and the short days plunged the entire western half of the state deeply into the doldrums. The park roster had at one time boasted two hundred members—men, women, and children, and sometimes four generations of families. The natural lake at the far end of the park, Lake Haussmann, was much too cold for anyone but the bravest (or the drunkest) to attempt swimming until mid-July, but it became one of the main social gathering spots when the temperature crept into the mid-seventies. Northwestern folk were a hardy lot, and since the warm season was so short, they found ways to extend it, which mostly included smiling a lot while shivering. One of the first things I noticed after moving here was that everybody seemed so much friendlier and generally happier than did those in California, despite the often inclement weather.

In its forty-five years or so of existence, membership at Deep Valley had declined significantly. Many long-term members had died and their children had lost interest in the park come their teenage years, when puberty and social pressure turned carefree children into gawky, self-conscious semi-adults who found their parents' lifestyle both embarrassing and a bit silly. The volleyball courts still stood as reminders of bygone days, but the sand had been invaded by weeds and the framework had begun to rust and crumble. The clubhouse roof leaked, creating giant brown spots in the ceiling. Rumors had begun to circulate that Deep Valley might be close to becoming financially insolvent. Without a transfusion of new blood and the membership dues that went along with it, Deep Valley would wither and die.

Eventually, fewer than one hundred die-hard members still remained, most of them noticeably grayer and paunchier than when they had started first taking off their clothes and entertaining themselves is various ways. Weekdays, the park was a ghost town, with the exception of a few "full-timers," some of whom hunkered down through the cold, wet, seemingly endless Northwest winters to once again emerge, as butterflies from chrysalises, pale but joyous nudists come the first sign of spring.

Grandma was one of the old-timers, an original member since 1975, when Wolfgang Haussmann, an immigrant and member of Germany's nudist community, and a few of Wolfgang's cronies bought the site on the cheap, pulled their trailers up, and began to plan for a community of like-minded folks that would eventually establish the only clothing-optional park between the

Canadian border and King County's Tiger Mountain Nudist Park, a short drive east from Seattle.

Today, Grandma was playing Bingo and drinking tea with several friends in the small town of Lyman, twenty minutes west of the park. At least that's what she had always told me when she left in the mornings. I knew better, though. Through the grapevine I had heard that her Bingo excursions were just a ruse. She was more than likely sampling whiskey and shooting skeet with several of her elderly friends. Alcohol, old age, and firearms may not have been an advisable combination, but who was I to judge a woman who had survived eighty-two years, two husbands, and stage III lung cancer?

Furthermore, she was kind enough to allow a grumbling, unemployed sot of a middle-aged man to share her home until he got back on his feet. I'd agreed to wash dishes, help with laundry, which was minimal, for obvious reasons, and assist with any repairs that were needed around the trailer and yard. Grandma's unusual diet consisted mainly of TV dinners and day-old donuts from Thrifty Foods, so dishwashing was minimal as well. I could never figure out how someone whose diet and lifestyle was so awful could have lived so long.

The trailer wasn't too shabby, for what it was, a rectangular metal tube with furniture. I couldn't complain. Grandma's trailer was one of the few truly permanent residences here at Deep Valley and a source of pride for her, humble though it was. At one time, her house was equipped with wheels and a license plate, but over the years it had sort of grown into the surrounding land, with a deck abutting an entire side, insulation underneath, and a covered porch Wolfgang had built on the other side. The interior was 1970's kitsch, replete with a collection of ceramic cats housed in a dusty cabinet, as well as a full set of those nesting Russian dolls. Grandma also had an odd obsession with tobacco pipes and frequently stood, coffee in hand, and stared through her thick coke-bottle glasses at possessions that would never again see the light of day. Just inside the entrance to the trailer sat a hulking after-market wood stove that roared all winter long, keeping the trailer not only bearable in the winter, but roughly eighty degrees Fahrenheit all year long, just the temperature Grandma liked. It was too hot for me, though, and I would fling open doors and windows in an attempt to get some fresh air. As soon as Grandma would arrive home in the afternoon, she would close them all and mutter discontentedly to herself.

With my Baileys and coffee warming my belly, I decided it was time to get a bit of exercise. I had spent more than enough time melting into the couch this week. I changed into some tennis shoes, stepped off the porch, and began a slow trudge around the two-mile inner circle of Deep Valley.

Dolores had finally finished her planting and had planted herself in her lawn chair, broad-brimmed hat down low over her face, shielding her from the sun, pendulous breasts flopping to either side of her chest, her ample belly going up and down as she drifted off for an afternoon nap. It was certainly a sight that took some getting used to but I felt a slight tinge of envy. Dolores didn't appear to give a single shit what anyone else thought of her.

On my leisurely trudge, I passed all manner of recreational vehicles, trailers, pop-up campers, and park models, some new and gleaming in the sun, others dull with moss accumulated over multiple rainy seasons. Elderly Winnebago trailers, their awnings askew, sat alongside sparkling new diesel motorhomes and classic Airstreams. A few club members sat in lawn chairs on their

7

porches or walking their lots aimlessly, drinks in hand. They all waved when I walked by. It was just like any other closely knit neighborhood, except that these neighbors were all naked. I must admit I did appreciate the congeniality of these folks; they seemed so much friendlier than the people in any other neighborhood I'd ever lived.

A low hum and the sound of crunching gravel heralded the approach of a golf cart from behind me. It seemed everyone owned one here, though, to my knowledge, nobody actually played golf. However, it was quick and easy transportation in a park where everything was spaced so closely together. The cart stopped to my left and an older man, wearing bright green knee-length shorts, his skin bronzed and leathery from years in the sun, said, "Hello neighbor!" and thrust out his hand.

The man possessed a firm handshake and continued shaking long after it seemed necessary. I smiled and gently pulled my hand back.

"Hi," I said.

"You're Clara's son, aren't you?"

"Grandson. Brian Bowman."

"Well, good to make your acquaintance, Brian Bowman. I'm Bob Haussmann. My dad started this place years ago. I'm the closest we've got to a security guard around here." Bob expelled a throaty smoker's guffaw, followed by a short episode of hacking.

When he had regained his composure, Bob continued. "So…" He looked me up and down, noting my baggy sweatshirt and faded green pajama bottoms. "Are you a textile?"

"Textile?" I was puzzled.

"That's what we call clothes-minded people."

I felt a tad taken aback. "I've never considered myself close-minded."

"Not close-minded," Bob said. "Clothes-minded." He exaggerated the "th" sound. "You know, like, you can't be seen naked?"

"Oh," I said, a bit relieved. "I've actually never thought about it."

Honestly, I hadn't really given nudism much thought. I wasn't exactly opposed to Grandma's lifestyle, or the folks with whom she kept company. The nudist lifestyle was just something to which I'd never paid much mind. Nudity for me was simply an interlude between episodes of wearing clothes, necessary for showering, sex, and the occasional examination in which you reveal all of yourself to your family physician. At any other time you cover up, so as not to be immodest. The idea of social nudity seemed foreign to me, perhaps even a bit silly. Grandma had always been a little more of a liberal persuasion, but became much more of a free spirit when she tired of my grandfather's philandering ways and left him many years ago. He died before the divorce was final. She had lived a nudist lifestyle ever since, but my parents had only chosen to visit her at the park in the winter, when even the die-hard nudists were bundled up under multiple layers of clothing, becoming reluctant textiles, braving the seemingly never-ending onslaught of gray, cold, northwest weather.

Grandma was never naked during visits from my family, a fact that I'm sure my father appreciated. She didn't seem to mind wearing clothes, which was just as well, because my father had no interest in his mother's odd hobby. Grandma had worn the same thick, pink bathrobe, seemingly, for decades, until the material wore thin and became translucent in places. Many at the park wore some sort of variation on the partially clothed theme, whether it be a bathrobe, a thick sweatshirt with a bare bottom, or sweatpants and no top. These were the winter nudist uniforms. Nothing ostentatious or even stylish. Just enough insulation to ward off the cold, while still maintaining the spirit of nudism.

"Sorry," said Bob. "Sometimes I toss around the nudist lingo a bit too freely. Don't mean to offend."

"No offense taken." I glanced at Bob's shorts and wondered why a nudist would feel compelled to cover one specific area of the body and not others. I refrained from questioning him, though.

"Well," said Bob. "Nice to meet you, Brian. I'm off to make my rounds. I'll catch you later!"

He sped off, leaving a cloud of dust in his wake. As his golf cart rattled off into the distance, I noticed an orange strobe light on its roof. I wondered if there were any security-related emergencies that would ever necessitate Bob's use of that light.

I trudged on, puffing up a slight incline and detected what I thought was the sound of giggling children. Around the bend was a vast grassy expanse punctuated by a tiny playground. A youngish man wearing a broad hat was reclined in a lawn chair, sipping a beverage. He waved as I approached.

"Hello neighbor!" he hollered as I came into view. Funny. It was the same greeting I'd just received from "Security Bob." I'd never met this fellow before.

I waved back and noticed that he was attempting, unsuccessfully, to supervise two squealing nude little girls who appeared identical. Neither of them wore a stitch of clothing as they slid gleefully down the rickety, sun-bleached, formerly red slide, chased each other around the surrounding sandbox, and pushed each other on swings.

I figured I'd saunter on over and introduce myself, hands shoved in my loose pockets. "I'm Brian."

Still seated in his lounge chair, the man extended his hand to shake. I must admit some initial trepidation as I wondered what he could have been doing with his hand just moments prior. Adjusting his genitals? Scratching his backside? With some hesitation and attempting to ignore my germophobia, I shook his hand. It was limp and moist. I reminded myself to wash my hands at the soonest possible opportunity.

"Mark," he replied. "These are my twin daughters, Mallory and Maddox." I smiled at the two children, who wore identical braids. They looked to be about six. The two paused briefly in their play to wave at me.

"Is this your first visit here?" asked Mark.

"No. I've been here for about two weeks. I'm staying with my grandmother, Clara."

"Oh!" A look of recognition crossed his face. "I think I'd heard about you. "Welcome. It's my weekend with these two. My ex-wife dropped them off yesterday. They just love it."

Mark, I was beginning to notice, was a rather unfortunate shape. With skinny, hairy legs, twig-like arms, and a ponderous belly, he had the misfortune of being both skinny and fat at the same time. I wondered if this could be me in a couple of years if I continued to slump further into inertia. He was also uncharacteristically pale for a nudist, his entire milky epidermis coated with a thick layer of sunscreen.

One of the two little girls walked over and tugged on her father's arm. "Daddy! Daddy!"

"What, Maddox?"

"Why is that man wearing clothes?"

"Well, Maddox. It's a clothing-optional park, so he can wear clothes if he wants to. It's his choice."

"Oh. Okay." Maddox seemed unfazed and went back to playing with Mallory.

"Sorry about that," said Mark. "She can't figure out why anybody would keep their clothes on here. I've tried to tell her before that everybody has a different comfort level and that it's okay to wear clothes."

"Perfectly okay," I said. "I don't mind at all. I guess I haven't made the great leap yet from textile to nudist." I watched as one of them—I'd already mixed them up—slid down the slide and landed with a plop in the sand. From my passing knowledge of the female anatomy, I surmised that nudity and sand might make for a rather uncomfortable combination.

Mark laughed. "Don't be in a rush. You'll get there in time. My ex-wife rejected my lifestyle, which might be one reason we're divorced."

"Sorry to hear that," I said.

"Don't be. It was for the best. I'm a lifelong nudist, maybe a little obsessive. Used to sneak out of the house at night when I was a kid and walk around the neighborhood nude with nobody the wiser but the raccoons. I'd climb trees, tromp around in the woods picking blackberries in the nude during the summers. Just had a grand old time. It's the best feeling in the world. Had to give it up and be responsible when I moved out of the house. Discovered this place about seven years ago and I've been a part-time resident ever since! The best part is, my daughters feel safe here. On any given weekend, they probably have about ten or fifteen honorary aunts and uncles looking out for them as well!"

It seemed from my brief interaction with him that Mark's enthusiasm for being naked might actually trump everything else in his life and it was a little difficult for me to relate. Even my love of science and the teaching thereof seemed to pale in comparison to Mark's starry-eyed ebullience at stripping his clothes off. Not really knowing what else to say, I replied, "Well, I'm going back to my walk. Nice to meet you," and continued my trudge.

"I'm in Trailer G7," said Mark. "Stop by some time!"

I didn't really plan to, as I wasn't particularly social, but I appreciated the gesture. I continued my walk around the circle, waving at my new neighbors if they waved at me, getting to know my new and unique environment. I was starting to feel a little more at home with each new neighbor I met. Grandma would soon be home, so I headed back to the trailer and started in on the dishes. But first I washed my hands.

A Visit to Grandma

I can remember being quite puzzled as a youngster of maybe seven or eight when the summer California heat beat down on us and I had asked my parents if we could visit Grandma up north. I knew it was noticeably cooler in Washington; our winter visits to Grandma's house were the only times I had ever seen snow and the inevitable slushy, muddy melt that followed days or even hours after a Seattle-area snowfall. Dad had rolled his eyes and mumbled something about it "not being a good time to visit Grandma."

I could recall only a handful of times my family and I had visited the park and seen Deep Valley as anything other than an ordinary campground. When I was ten and visiting Grandma over the Christmas and New Year's holiday, she had invited us to the clubhouse for an evening potluck. Club members milled about in street clothes or fluffy bathrobes, paper plates of hors d'oeuvres in their hands. The fireplace crackled warmly, its mantel bedecked by wreaths. A Christmas tree stood in the corner. It seemed like any other neighborhood gathering. At one point, however, an elderly couple had wandered into the clubhouse naked, towels slung over their shoulders, steam rising off their backs, presumably just having exited the adjacent hot tub. They also appeared a bit tipsy, weaving slightly, empty plastic wine glasses held loosely in their arthritic fingers. Glass, for obvious reasons, was not allowed in the hot tub area. The elderly gent and his wife placed their towels on nearby chairs, greeted their neighbors warmly, and sat.

I had turned to my mother, who appeared to be shading her face with a paper dinner plate. "Do those people know they're naked?" I whispered.

"Well, um…" she stammered. "Not everybody wears clothes here. It's a Nudist Park."

"Nudist Park…" I repeated. Well, that did sound like fun, but there was no way I could ever be naked in public. I cast furtive glances at the two naked elders, their skin loose and pale. I contemplated the skin of my own hands, supple and tan. Was this my future?

At one point, Grandma caught my gaze and appeared amused. "You embarrassed, Brian?" She cackled. I reddened.

"That's Howard and Nancy," said Grandma. "Two of our oldest members. Nice people. I'll introduce you."

"Um, no thank you," I mumbled.

Howard and Nancy continued to drink and laugh and appeared not to have a care in the world as they conversed with their friends and played cards. When they got up to leave, a bit unsteadily, I noticed that Nancy's nipples seemed to be about even with her belly button.

Grandma was never one who could be considered a die-hard nudist. Even in sultry August, she had worn some kind of a cover-up, whether it be a sarong around her waist, a pair of shorts without a top, or one of many extra-long T-shirts. For her, the social aspect of club life was just as important as the privilege of being

15

able to walk around naked. It was all about being comfortable to her.

One summer, however, rumor has it she had chosen to spend her seventy-fifth birthday in grand style at the park, wearing nothing but a pair of Birkenstock sandals and a green sun visor. Her sense of freedom and overall joie de vivre was likely encouraged by the fact that by noon she had consumed, by herself, an entire bottle of gin and three Coors Lights kindly but unwisely given to her by her friends.

With an ear-to-ear grin, a gin and tonic in one hand, and a cigarette in the other, she had made her rounds in her gold cart, visiting all her friends, careening joyfully, if a bit recklessly, from one trailer to another. At one point, she had gone off-road, or off-trail in any case, and ended up mowing down Dolores's flower bed, a fact for which she apologized profusely the following evening, only after it was pointed out by Bob Haussmann. Grandma herself had no recollection of the event.

Grandma's grand seventy-fifth culminated at about seven o'clock that evening with her falling off her porch while telling an amusing story. She hadn't been injured, aside from a scratch or two, but did experience grass and twigs in and adhered to parts of her anatomy where she wasn't accustomed to having such things. She was promptly put to bed by her friends.

LISA TAKES A DIP

Lisa Cato was just completing her sixth lap around Lake Hauss-mann, feeling winded but exhilarated at the same time. She ran to the tempo of her breath as her new pink tennis shoes crunched on the loose gravel. A cool breeze ruffled her long blond hair, and she relished the feeling of her unfettered breasts jiggling as she jogged. They were small, pert, and round and didn't necessitate a sports bra. At least Lisa didn't think so. Most men around the park would also agree that she didn't need a bra, or shouldn't wear one, though they were careful to look into her eyes when they spoke to her. A woman with Lisa's looks and youth was like a four-leaf clover at a nudist park largely populated by chunky mid-dle-aged men.

Lisa checked her pulse as she ran, counting the pulsations of her carotid artery against the sports watch she wore on her left wrist: 160. She was in the zone, and nearing the end of her daily five-mile jog. Her reward was in sight—a dip in the chilly waters of Lake Haussmann.

As she jogged towards the rustic clubhouse that marked the end of her run, heart rate beginning to slow, a couple approached from the opposite direction, both nude, making their way very slowly around the lake. The man appeared to be in his eighties, stooped over and leaning heavily on a cane, his skin white, almost opaque, contrasting with the dark tan of his accomplice, a gray-haired woman who appeared to be strong and healthy, but who walked at the pace of her partner. The man steadied himself by keeping a hand on her elbow as he strode with the cane in his other hand. The old man smiled at Lisa as she jogged past, and she noticed that the woman was carrying a bag containing crusts of bread. They had been feeding the many ducks that congregated at one end of the lake in a reedy area. Lisa smiled back. It was nice to see older members still getting out for a walk on such a brilliant day, though she wasn't particularly happy about encountering the duck poop inherent in the overfed flock that had made Lake Haussmann their home. They man and woman were the eldest of elders in this community of mostly middle-aged and retired folk. Lisa and the couple were on opposite ends of the age spectrum in the nudist community. At twenty-eight, Lisa was a rarity as one of the under-forty crowd, but she was hardly a neophyte. She and her family had been coming to the park for twenty-five years. She'd grown up here and had swam in Lake Haussmann since she was small.

As Lisa approached the clubhouse, her pace slowed to a stop. She placed her hands on her hips, chest heaving. She paced for a few seconds in the grass surrounding the clubhouse, allowing her heart rate to reduce. Perspiration glistened on her forehead, breasts, and supple inner thighs.

Lisa sat in the cool, damp grass and removed her shoes, sweaty socks, and watch. She'd ruined more than one non-waterproof watch in her exuberance to plunge into the water. Leaving her belongings in a pile in the grass—she knew nobody would even think of stealing her things here—Lisa strode the short distance across the grass to the dock that stretched several yards off into the water. On the "beach," a few folks basked on their towels, gazed at their phones, or read books. A couple of preschool-aged kids waded out into a silty, shallow area near the dock under the watchful eyes of their parents.

The floating dock shifted under Lisa's bare feet and she felt butterflies of anticipation. There was nothing better than a cool lake on a warm summer day. With childlike abandon, she leaped into the still water and made a most undignified splash. Lisa was no diver, but she swam like an eel, undulating through the murky water with an unconventional but powerful side to side motion. The cold made her gasp for a moment, but then, recovering, she dunked her head in the water and propelled herself out a ways from the dock, relishing the complete freedom of swimming un-inhibited by clothing. If it was possible, Lisa felt even more naked than when she had been running, feeling the water envelop every inch of her body. She loved it.

After she joyfully splashed around a bit, Lisa hoisted herself onto the dock. She shivered and wrung out her long hair. She gazed down at her small nipples, erect from the cold, nearly hard enough to cut glass. She decided to lie out for a while on the dock and let the sun dry her. She knew it wouldn't be long before she was warm again. It had been so long since she had worn a swimming suit, she couldn't really remember the first time she swam without one, the feeling of no longer having a clingy piece of fabric that retained water stuck to her skin. There really was nothing better than swimming in the buff. It was only natural.

After a few minutes of glorious sunbathing, Lisa arose, slowly, so as not to give herself a head rush. She had quite low blood pressure, so fainting was always a possibility, especially in this heat. She ambled over to her belongings, exactly where she had left them, and put them back on. It was now time to walk home, make herself a protein shake, and take her customary noon nap.

President Grandma

The clattering of the flimsy screen door announced Grandma's
return from her outing. I had been dozing on her overstuffed
couch, but she didn't seem to notice as she flung her car keys onto
the counter and then plopped herself down next to me. She
grabbed the television remote from between the seat cushions and
waved it to and fro, as though she was conducting a symphony.

"Goddammit," she muttered, as the TV refused to respond to
her requests.

"Afternoon, Grandma," I said, and opened one bleary eye.

"Oh!" said Grandma. "Were you sleeping?"

"Just resting," I lied. There was a lot that Grandma didn't notice. "How was your uh…Bingo?"

"Lovely." She fumbled with a hearing aid and smoothed her
gray hair over her right ear. It was a nervous gesture that I'd come
to recognize. "Brian, what's this?" She picked up my coffee cup
and sniffed it. "Tsk tsk. Alcohol? It isn't even two o'clock yet."

"That's never stopped you, Grandma."

More smoothing and hearing aid fumbling. I knew she was
pretending she couldn't hear me. The hearing aid chirped, so I
knew it was on. Grandma had a habit of turning her hearing aids
off at times and sitting in blissful oblivion to the conversations

going on around her. She slurped up the remains of my morning beverage. Any time was a suitable happy hour for Grandma.

However, other than the selective deafness, Grandma took it upon herself to be aware of all the goings-on in the park: whose wife hadn't visited in months, whose dog was currently on the naughty list for wandering onto other lots and pooping, what couples seemed to be surreptitiously trading spouses. Grandma even seemed to be aware of the petty squabbles that took place between couples in what they thought was the privacy of their own trailers.

Grandma made all this her business, partly because she was a self-admitted busybody, but also because she was the president of Deep Valley Family Nudist Park, a position she took very seriously. She chaired the Deep Valley Club Council, a group of four that held great clout in the park. As president, she had the ultimate authority for approving or disapproving new members, and the power to terminate someone's membership for any of several violations listed in the member handbook, among them, no drunken golf cart driving, no showcasing of one's erect genitalia, and no outright lewd behavior.

It wasn't all order and seriousness, though. On weekends, Grandma presided over the club's weekly karaoke nights, held in the clubhouse. The amplification system, purchased recently by a club member with significant resources and donated to the club, was so powerful it could be heard over the entire park and beyond, so that when Grandma took the mic herself, usually well into her cups by then, and belted out Dusty Springfield's "Son of a Preacher Man" at eleven p.m., nobody in the park was able to get much sleep. Dorothy and Art's tiny terrier, Charlie, howled in accompaniment. Ole Gustafson, who was eighty and opposed to fun, often walked in, looked pained, and then wandered off to his trailer. A great time was had by most.

At the beginning of every spring, Grandma headed the park clean-up day, which was actual work for some of the more able-bodied members, but a time of socialization, reminiscing, coffee drinking, and the occasional deadheading of shrubs for the older folks, most of whom came for the free food. The weed whackers and lawnmowers emerged from storage and the more sensible members wore clothes. At the end of the day, the park looked slightly better than it had before, and participating members were treated to the yearly Deep Valley Weenie Roast. The joke, in this case, was so obvious nobody bothered to mention it.

After a few seconds of frantic remote-waving, Grandma was finally successful in her endeavors and soon happily ensconced in the daytime drama of "Judge Judy." She pulled a cigarette out of a new pack, fumbled for a lighter, failed to find one, and then fell asleep, the unlit cig loosely held between her first and second fingers.

With nothing much else to do, I dozed off as well, face-down, my nose squashed against a tobacco-infused decorative pillow and one arm around another. I was simply too lazy to make my way to the bedroom for a proper nap.

After an hour or so, I awoke to the afternoon sun beaming through the western-facing windows and the rather jarring sound of Grandma's gravelly cigarette voice as she shouted into the telephone.

"What? Again? That's the second time this week!" There was a pause as she waited for the person on the other end of the line to finish ranting in a high-pitched and screechy voice. "I know, Helen. I'll handle it."

Grandma put the mobile phone down on the table with an irritated clunk. She located a lighter which had fallen between the couch and the table, hastily lit her cigarette, took a drag, and then exhaled smoke through her nose while simultaneously sighing in an annoyed fashion.

"Brian, you awake?"

"I am now."

"I've got official business to take care of, and I need your help."

I lifted my head off the pillow, propped myself up on one elbow, and rubbed my eyes. "What's up?"

"Melvin and Janet are at in again."

"At what, exactly?"

"Wasting water in the middle of summer, that's what. Come on, I need you as the intimidation factor." Grandma slipped into a pair of worn Birkenstocks and began toddling towards the door.

"Intimidation factor? How?"

"Never mind how! Let's go. We'll take the golf cart."

I arose quite suddenly, felt light-headed, then followed Grandma out the door and into her golf cart. For an old lady, she could certainly move fast when she had a mission.

I sat down beside her on a towel of questionable hygiene that she kept there for when her naked friends accompanied her on jaunts around the park. The cart rumbled over gravel and potholes, jarring us repeatedly as I remained mystified as to the mission I was being sent on.

Grandma turned sharply around a corner and pulled the cart to a halt with a screech and a cloud of dust in front of a lot upon which a massive fifth wheel trailer was perched on a grassy hillside. She hoisted herself out with a groan.

"I'll do all the talking," she said. "Brian, you just stand there with your arms folded and look like you mean business."

Completely bemused by the situation, I followed Grandma a few paces and then stood as told, arms folded, dark sunglasses covering my eyes. How a chubby, 5'8" college professor wearing a pair of ragged pajama bottoms was meant to look intimidating, I wasn't sure.

There, at the top of the hillside, stood a Rubenesque septuagenarian sporting a broad grin, a broad pink sun hat, and nothing else but the skin she was born with. Beside her was a tarp that extended from the top of the hill, at least twenty feet down to the bottom. A garden hose gurgled away at the top, spewing water down to a small pool formed by excess tarp at the bottom.

Grandma stood and watched as a thin, naked elderly man picked up what appeared to be a bottle of dish detergent and squatted down to drizzle some of its contents onto the tarp, his back turned, his droopy scrotum waggling about. I winced. Grandma frowned.

The old man stepped away and the woman plopped her ample behind onto the tarp. The man gave her a mighty shove and she was off.

"Wee!" she squealed as she shot down the hillside on the tarp, landing with a considerable splash in the soapy pool.

Grandma cleared her throat. "Ahem! Janet and Melvin!"

The couple looked startled and then almost immediately sheepish. The woman, Janet presumably, stiffened and removed her hat as she stood in the soapy pool.

"I'm pretty sure I've mentioned this to you before, "said Grandma. "No slip n slides. We're in a water shortage."

Janet hung her head. "Sorry, Clara. Won't happen again." She splashed forlornly out of the pool and made her way soggily up the hill. Melvin echoed his wife's apology, turned off the hose, and then sank into a lawn chair before cracking open a beer from a cooler that sat near his chair and a chaise with a pink towel draped over it. Janet finished puffing up the hill and then beached herself on the chaise. The two were clearly determined to enjoy the day, slip n slide or not.

"You two have fun," said Grandma, before settling herself back into the golf cart.

Melvin tipped his beer. "You too, Clara."

"I'm all for folks havin' fun," said Grandma, "but you gotta abide by the rules. Last time them two did that, they got a little tipsy and forgot to turn off the hose until the evening. They turned the next lot into a swamp. Gunter went to mow the lawn the next day and sank in it. We had to winch the mower out."

I chuckled.

"Not funny, Brian. Gunter's got a little bit of a weight problem and we had to winch him out too."

At that statement I burst into laughter, mentally picturing a large naked man being dragged to safety through mud via a winch. Grandma boggled at me through her thick glasses and then began laughing herself.

"I guess it is kind of funny," she said finally. "He's pretty accident prone. Last summer he drove his golf cart off the road and into the blackberry bushes. Three of us had to help that poor son of a bitch out of the ditch. Looked like his naked ass had been attacked by a family of porcupines! Took him a couple days to get all the thorns out."

I didn't stop laughing until we made it back to the trailer and Grandma had parked the golf cart. Uproarious laughter was so uncharacteristic of me, but somehow minor calamities seemed so much funnier when I pictured the victim naked.

"Anyway," said Grandma, "thanks for going with me."

"I'm not sure how I helped. There's nothing even vaguely intimidating about me."

"You're taller'n me by a foot. I needed those two to know I meant business."

THE REVEREND

The Reverend Dale Parkhurst scowled as he gazed out of his living-room window. He and his wife had built the five-bedroom, 4500-square-foot structure on five acres to be their retirement home, a place of reflection and solitude, a respite from the misguided and sinful world surrounding them. At sixty-six, he was still working as the full-time rector of Grace Church of God, and planned to be at it for some time to come. He had just come in from church after preaching his usual marathon back to back to back services, starting at 0600 in the morning.

Reverend Dale was tired, and he was not enjoying his view in the least. The last thing he wanted to see was naked people below, basking like iguanas beside Lake Haussmann, occasionally flipping over from front to back, like burgers on a grill. Dale removed his eyeglasses from atop their perch on his elaborately coiffed but thinning gray pate and placed them on the bridge of his nose where his vision was best. Yep, definitely naked people. He thought he saw a penis.

Over the winter, on days when the rain abated for a while, Dale loved to sip his morning coffee and look out over Lake Haussmann, named for a nudist pioneer, so pristine, the water still as glass. The leaves had fallen from the surrounding trees, offering Dale an unobstructed view of the placid expanse. Nary a soul was in sight in the winter, with the exception of the funny little man who drove the golf cart with the orange light on the top, and he was always bundled up in a thick parka. His usual routine was to drive his cart to the edge of the lake, get out and walk to the end of the dock, puffing on a cigarette, pondering the view. Dale disapproved of the smoking, but it was certainly preferable to the immorality of public nudity to which he so often had to be subjected. Something should be done.

The indomitable and ever-cheery Jan Parkhurst emerged from the bedroom, having just changed out of her pastor's wife ensemble and into a comfortable sweatshirt and pair of sweatpants. Her enthusiasm for her husband's fervent religiosity had waned in recent years, though she still maintained the façade of a faithful preacher's wife, always at his side for the many public functions he attended, smiling broadly though inside she was dying. If she had the courage, she would have left long ago to pursue decidedly unchristian adventures.

"Dale, how long are you going to stare out that window? You haven't moved since I went into the bedroom."

Interrupted in his fuming reverie, Dale startled and nearly dropped his coffee. "Lord in Heaven, Jan, give me some warning next time before you sneak up behind me."

"The naked people are out there again, huh?" Jan found her husband's ire amusing.

Dale set his coffee cup down hard on the counter as though he were a judge banging a gavel. "Yes, Jan," he said, enunciating each word as though he were explaining something to a small child. "The naked people are out there again."

"Why do you let it bother you so much?"

Now this was really something that galled him. For a preacher's wife, she should have a better understanding of the immorality of nudity in mixed company and the need for modest dress at all times. And what about the children? He wasn't sure if children were allowed at the park, but he certainly hoped not. After all, Dale and Jan had grandchildren. In fact, they would be visiting next month, in the heat of the summer, and Dale hadn't yet thought of a way to divert their attention from the view of the lake. Surely, they would want to play on the property. Jackson and Haydon loved to climb trees. What if they looked over the bluff and saw a naked person? Perish the thought.

"It bothers me because, well it…" He stumbled for the words. "It's just not right what they are doing down there."

"Dear, why don't you sit down and I'll make us some brunch."

"And how am I supposed to eat my sausage and eggs with…with phalluses and breasts outside my window?"

"Phalli, Dale, and they aren't just outside your window. You'd need binoculars to make out any features at all. Either you have the vision of an eagle or you're just getting yourself all worked up over a non-problem. Probably both. Let it go for now."

Binoculars. Now that was an idea he hadn't thought of. And he wasn't about to let it go. His dream house, surrounded by a nudist colony. When was Jesus going to come back and right this wrong, punish the sinners and the whores and the Sodomites?

His sausage and eggs now steaming in front of him, Dale violently stabbed at them with a fork and continued to fume internally. He didn't like the idea of having nudists for neighbors, and he certainly didn't appreciate his wife's attempts to placate him.

BRIAN NEEDS A JOB

Monday morning reared its ugly head, bringing with it the usual hangover. I ran my tongue over my dry lips and tasted something reminiscent of the ass end of a camel. I could never remember to brush my teeth prior to bed if I had had something to drink, which was, of course, every night. Or perhaps it wasn't so much that I had forgotten, but that I had passed out altogether after a night of whiskey and Coke multiplied many times over. The worst of it was the Coke, or the Dr. Pepper, or whatever it was that Grandma had on hand, that made my head throb and bombilate with each attempt to lift my head from the pillow.

Moderation was not my forte, unfortunately, though I attempted to comfort myself by reminding myself that I had been even less functional at the university, studying molecular biology and organic chemistry. Most days I would trudge to class blearily, eyes burning, head throbbing, and attempt to absorb some scintilla of information from the lectures. Some days I didn't go to class at all. I could only credit a fair amount of native cerebral horsepower—my IQ was once measured at 145—that allowed me to graduate at all and continue on to graduate school. My grades were not stellar, but the dean of the College of Arts and Sciences at the University of Washington was intrigued by the research I had done on the Northern Alligator Lizard, one of the very few we have on the damp side of the state. It wasn't exactly earth-shattering research, but it was sufficiently interesting and different in the world of academia.

Today would be the first day I would go in search of some sort of gainful employment. The university had given me a generous severance package but it would only last another eight weeks or so, less if I drank a good percentage of it. I wasn't eligible for unemployment as the termination officially went down as a resignation. The clock was ticking.

It was true that my university lecture position took a lot out of me—late nights preparing lectures, grading examinations, and the office hours before and after lectures—but I loved to teach. I liked to say I hated my job, but I loved what I did.

I had an appointment to meet with a faculty member at Skagit Valley College in Mount Vernon to see if I could secure an intermittent position as a substitute lecturer and possibly accrue more hours by assisting with labs. At first blush, community college teaching seemed to be a step down for me, but it was where I had originally started my career, first with a master's degree and later with my Ph.D. I enjoyed the students and found them to be every bit as smart as those I taught at a state university. The pay wasn't optimal, but without rent, my overhead was significantly lower. I figured that if didn't pull myself up by my bootstraps sooner rather than later, I would lose traction.

With difficulty, I arose from bed and headed to the tiny bathroom to complete my daily routine, teeth brushed for exactly two minutes including the tongue, five swipes of deodorant per underarm, then shave all but my graying goatee. As I urinated, swaying slightly and bracing myself on the wall, I regretted not drinking more water. However, regret was something I experienced on a daily basis. Unfortunately, it had little effect on my behavior.

My clothes for the day had been perfectly folded and neatly laid out on a desk in my room by a slightly more sober version of myself who had been quite functional until about six o'clock the previous night. Grandma did the ironing, for which I was grateful, but had a habit of balling the clothes up after the fact in an attempt to fold them, thus defeating the purpose. Therefore, I had insisted on doing the folding and the putting away.

As I straightened my tie with slightly shaking fingers, I gazed outside through the dingy window. As was often the case with our Pacific Northwest summers, the sun had not yet made an appearance, choosing instead to hide behind the dense cumulus clouds until it felt the time was right, usually about two o'clock in the afternoon or so, when everybody had given up and made other plans for the day.

Much like the sun, Grandma spent many a morning wrapped up in her own personal cumulus clouds, a plethora of quilts and down comforters underneath which peacefully snored a little old lady who weighed no more than one hundred twenty pounds. I could hear her sonorous breathing even through the shut door and was thankful for the ear plugs I wore at night. She would probably be up by noon to sit out on her porch and smoke a cigarette, before walking up to the office to chat with the staff. At her age, I figured, she deserved to take it easy.

Next, to feel more like a human being and less like a pile of owl dung, I needed coffee. I trudged out to the kitchen and opened every cabinet I could find that might contain a bag, box or a pod. Even a plastic container of Folger's would suffice at this point. I knew Grandma drank coffee by the pot as it went so well with her Marlboro Lights. After looking even so far as underneath the sink with all the cleaning supplies and finding not a single coffee bean, I decided to give up and get going.

The screen door that was never locked clattered shut behind me and I walked down the aged steps of Grandma's house and opened the door to my silver 2018 Prius, soon to be a relic from my days of relative financial security. I hoped not to sell it, but if I didn't find a way to get back on my feet, I wouldn't even have the shirt on my back. Thankfully, I didn't have to drive Grandma's ancient Plymouth Fury, her "jalopy" that belched blue smoke upon start-up and eventually coughed itself to life like an old smoker arising from bed to start the day. I had often wondered which one would go first, Grandma or her "jalopy." My bets were on the jalopy.

As I approached the final curve to exit the park, I remembered that it was past eight o'clock and the office would be open. I hoped that the coffee pot was on. The woman that usually opened and closed the office on weekdays, Helen, was an amply sized older woman with a preference for flowered dresses so tight that she appeared not so much dressed as upholstered. By herself, she would usually down a pot of coffee and any donuts that hadn't been eaten by visitors after noon. She was friendly enough, but not so easy on the eyes.

I parked at the office, little more than a portable building half the size of Grandma's trailer. I left the engine running; I didn't plan to stay long. Splash and dash. Security Bob was just traipsing down the steps and getting into his golf cart as I approached. He waved and said hello.

As I opened the sliding glass door, the delicious aroma of freshly brewed coffee wafted towards me. On shelves in the office rested coffee cups for sale, emblazoned with the logo of Deep Valley Nudist Park. A row of Deep Valley Nudist Park T-shirts and tank tops in all conceivable colors hung on hangers along the wall. I'd seen them there before and had been rather baffled as to why clothing was on sale in an establishment that seemed to eschew the very concept of unnecessary fabric. Several stacks of magazines were neatly piled on an adjacent shelf, their covers depicting young, smiling nude men and women playing volleyball or kayaking a placid lake. A small television chattered to itself from a bracket on the wall.

At first I didn't see anybody standing behind the desk but I did see my goal, the coffee pot and stack of cups sitting on the counter beside a sign-up sheet and open laptop computer. I approached and peered over the counter. Indeed there was a front desk attendant wearing a flowered dress, bent over and rummaging through a cardboard box that was labeled "communications."

"Bob, where are the radios?" came a voice from the person crouched behind the counter. I still hadn't seen her face. She muttered to herself. Hearing no answer, she called again, "Bob, have you seen the radios?"

The figure began to straighten and turn around. I realized fairly quickly that she didn't much resemble Helen.

"Oh hello," I said.

The attendant looked to be in her mid-twenties. Her hair was platinum blond. She had a deep tan and piercing blue eyes. Around her neck she wore a gold chain with a small cross. The dress she wore was form-fitting and hugged her in all the right places. She seemed startled to see me.

"Hi!" she exclaimed. "Thought Bob was still here. Sorry. I'm Lisa." She extended a hand.

I shook her hand. "I'm Brian. Just thought I might find some coffee here?"

"Oh yeah! We've always got coffee." She gestured to the coffee pot and a small box beside it. "And creamer and sugar. Whatever you need. Are you new here?"

"I am. Clara is my grandmother. I'm just staying here for a while." I helped myself to some coffee.

"Yeah? I love Clara!"

This new girl was certainly bubbly, and much more fun to chat with than the monotone, seemingly perpetually depressed Helen.

"Yeah, she's…something, all right," I said, trying to come up with the words to sum up my often cranky but ever-generous grandmother.

"So, what brings you to our little Garden of Eden, Brian?" Lisa cocked her head to the side and brushed a stray lock of blond hair from her face. Was she flirting? I was never able to figure out women, especially when it came to subtle hints. It was no small wonder I had ever gotten married in the first place.

"Long story, Lisa. Just looking for a change, I guess." That was a complete lie. Telling the truth in a situation like this seemed easier said than done. My response certainly sounded better than, "Lost my job because I'm a drunk, then got kicked out of my house, because my soon-to-be ex-wife agrees with the university."

"Hmmmmm." I could tell she wasn't buying it. "Well, cool then! Welcome!"

I sipped my coffee. Bland and watered down but marginally palatable. "Thank you. I've enjoyed it here so far. So uh…are you the office manager?"

"Oh shit no." Lisa laughed and then clapped her hands to her mouth. "Oops. Oh my God. I'm so sorry. I've got a little bit of a swearing problem." She reddened, her gaze downcast. "Nah, I just help out here from time to time. I'm a second-generation Deep Valley Member."

"No offense taken. My mouth has gotten me in trouble on many occasions. Well, I've got a job interview so I need to get going. Nice to meet you." Another thing about beautiful women is that they distract me to the point of being non-functional. I left my coffee cup steaming on the counter.

The Great Unraveling

As I drove westbound on Highway 20 towards Mount Vernon, out of the verdant foothills so often socked in with fog but now bathed in brilliant sunlight, I reflected on what I had come to refer to as The Great Unraveling of my life. My real troubles had started long before my unfortunate termination from the college, though that was the icing on the cake to the week from Hell.

My wife, Jennifer, and I had had a difficult relationship for some time. To say nothing of the fact that we came from diametrically opposed family backgrounds, we each worked ourselves to the bone and found little time for each other. The demands of my teaching post, the off-hour research, and the drive to attain tenure as a full professor drove a wedge between us. Jennifer worked in real estate and was often called away for a showing even when we had had something planned for the evening. Within a few years, we had become total strangers.

We had met on a blind date and had become instantly attracted to each other, but it was difficult to pinpoint many other points of commonality besides a mutual appreciation for each other's physique and a shared love of cheesy 90's sitcoms, as well as a disdain for organized religion. We seemed to survive on this alone for about two years, but when the initial attraction faded, we were left with nothing more than mere familiarity and the occasional lackluster late-night coupling. Jennifer never wanted children, in fact I think she despised them. This should have been one of my first clues that things wouldn't work out. I wasn't willing yet to commit to a childless future. It was something we probably should have discussed prior to plunging into marriage, debt, and, ultimately, mediocrity.

Jennifer and I differed in other ways as well. While I was perfectly content to shuffle about in ill-fitting, baggy sweatpants and moth-eaten T-shirts, Jennifer was obsessed with appearance, seemingly eating up hours of her days and evenings examining every blemish, every fine line, and every gray hair on her head. She dressed impeccably, as was befitting of a woman whose profession demanded it and carried that mien with her even after her workday was done. At first she had reacted with annoyance to my casual dress, my unkempt hair, and my scroungy beard, but after a time, she didn't seem to care.

In all the time we had been married, I believe I had seen her naked twice, both times as she emerged from the shower. She had quickly wrapped herself in a towel and retreated to the walk-in closet like some kind of refuge from the lecherous man that lived in her house. Sex, when it occurred, which was rarely, was a puritanical event we engaged in with the room pitch dark - at her insistence of course - and her pajama bottoms pulled down to mid-thigh. Usually sex was my idea, and more than once I thought to check Jennifer's neck for a pulse mid-coitus as she was about as active in bed as a tortoise on Quaaludes.

Alcohol snuck in, incrementally, subtly, but steadily, into my off time. A drink or two in the evening to wind down devolved into sometimes consuming an entire fifth of whiskey in one sitting. My trips to the corner store became more frequent. The clerks began to know me by name.

On several occasions, I was not only hungover but still slightly drunk upon arriving at work. The jug of mouthwash in my desk drawer became my friend, and I maintained for quite some time—maybe months.

Jennifer left on a Tuesday and the rent was due on a Wednesday, the first of the month. She had withdrawn half the money from our joint account and placed it in her own, separate account. She didn't return my phone calls, so I had to rely on the last month's rent I had paid when we had moved into the apartment. I had needed to find a new place in a matter of weeks.

What else was there to do but to drink my sorrows away? Friday I came to work physically but not mentally. Had I been pulled over by the police on the way in, I would likely have been arrested for DUI. My first lecture was a shambles. After becoming utterly confused by the laptop I had been using for years to project PowerPoint presentations, I had resorted to the white dry-erase board. After having scribbled some diagrams on the topic of vertebrate embryology that may or may not have made any sense, I turned around to meet the shocked expressions of many of the students. What in the hell had happened to Professor Bowman? No longer able to hide my "secret" affliction, I hastily answered a few questions and then dismissed the class. I wasn't feeling well, I said. Everyone was welcome to take the rest of the hour off and study for the exam on Monday.

Monday came and a relatively sober Brian walked into the lecture hall, hoping to re-establish my competence as an instructor. There to greet me at the door was Dr. Henry Yonemitsu, dean of the Biology Department. He looked grim and asked me to accompany him to his office.

"Shut the door behind you please and have a seat," he said.

Shaking, I closed the door and took a seat. Then I noticed University President Mary McEwen seated next to Henry's desk. This certainly didn't look like it was shaping up to be a friendly chat.

"Brian," Dr. Yonemitsu began, clearing his throat. "We need to discuss something very difficult. Dr. McEwen is here as well per protocol for…these sorts of things."

My heart thumped in my chest.

"Your recent erratic behavior, together with your chronic tardiness to meetings or failure to attend meetings at all, um…doesn't meet the standards of this university." He looked uncomfortable, focusing on the desk in front of him and gestured hopelessly at President McEwen.

President McEwen was more direct. "Brian, we are aware you have a drinking problem. We have known it for some time. As you will recall, there was a similar issue in 2015 for which we recommended alcohol rehabilitation, which you completed. However, you seem to have relapsed. We've given you chance after chance and we're at the end of the line here. Historically, you have been a great asset to the faculty, but in all fairness to the students, we can't keep you on. Dr. Yonemitsu and I are in agreement. We are going to have to let you go."

There was little to say. The decision had been made. There was some paperwork to fill out, a desk to empty, and some pictures and diplomas to remove from the walls. Just like that, I was out. No job, no wife, and soon-to-be no home.

I drove home in a fugue, parked my car in its usual spot, walked into my apartment, and…you guessed it, made myself a drink. My very next phone call was to Grandma, who then graciously extended me the offer to live with her for a while and welcomed me with open arms when I arrived.

My reverie was interrupted by an eighteen-wheeler from British Columbia threatening to reduce me and my vehicle to two-dimensional status. I accelerated rapidly and regained my grip on reality. Within minutes, I was off the freeway and pulling into the parking lot of Skagit Valley College.

The job interview went reasonably well, I thought. It was an informal affair, little more than a chat with the department head in the cafeteria over a cup of coffee. Diane Schenck, a professor who had done Ph.D. research similar to my own, had an easy manner and an ever-present smile that only faded slightly when I informed her of the circumstances surrounding my departure from my university post. I was as honest as I could be in admitting to my problems and promised that I would never let my students down like that again.

In the end, Dr. Schenck handed me an application and said that she was sure she could get me some regular hours as a lab assistant and that the students would greatly benefit from my experience and education. As for lectures, she said it came down to my being available with very little notice when sick calls arose. Dr. Schenck assured me that teaching opportunities would increase significantly come fall quarter. Two elderly instructors were on the fence as to whether or not they would come back to teach in the fall, one of whom was considering medical retirement due to long-term illness. A warm handshake and a smile concluded the informal interview, and I left feeling buoyed for the first time in a long time.

I nearly skipped out to my car and considered the possibility that I might actually be able to keep it. A light rain fell, unusual for July, but I didn't much mind. The tiny drops felt good on my head. The trip back to Deep Valley from Mount Vernon was pleasant and relatively traffic-free.

TROUBLE FOR GRANDMA

As my car rounded the final curve towards Grandma's trailer, I spotted the first emergency vehicle, an SUV with more blinking lights than a Christmas tree, parked at Grandma's neighbor's house. What was truly disturbing, though, was the ambulance backed directly in front of the ramp that led to Grandma's front door, its rear doors open. My heart sank. What had happened to Grandma?

My usual parking spot blocked, I put the car into park, slammed shut the door, and ran up the ramp to find Skagit County Fire District #8's EMTs loading Grandma onto a stretcher. I was briefly obstructed by an elderly roadblock called "Linda Berg, Battalion Chief." At least that's what the gold name plate affixed to her white uniform shirt read. The woman appeared to have been working in the fire service since God was a small child and clutched a clipboard in her hand. It appeared to be her sole responsibility. After saying "excuse me" twice, the chief wearily ceded her space on the ramp and moved to the side.

I recognized Dorothy and Art's terrier Charlie spinning in circles in the front yard, chasing his tiny tail and failing to catch it.

"Grandma, what happened?"

"Brian, I tripped over that frigging dog!" She pointed with her unlit cigarette, indicating the tiny terrier. "They say I might have broken my hip. I have to go to Skagit Hospital." Grandma fumbled with a lighter.

"Ma'am. You can't smoke," said a young, red-haired man with a beard and goatee.

"Come on guys. It'll be my last smoke afore I'm laid up in the hospital."

The EMT shrugged. "Sorry, ma'am. Those are the rules."

The EMS crew clicked the seatbelts on the gurney in preparation for transporting Grandma to the hospital. Her unlit cigarette still dangled between her first and second fingers. She winced as they raised the stretcher to the load position. Beneath her left leg was a pillow. It looked like the EMTs had also tied her legs together with some sort of bandaging material.

As they wheeled Grandma down the ramp and into the waiting ambulance, a young woman, clad in firefighter pants with suspenders, followed them out, carrying a tablet computer. I recognized her as the same woman I had met this morning at the office—Lisa.

"Brian, right?" she said as she gathered medical bags and hefted them onto her shoulder.

"Yes. Lisa?"

She smiled. "Right. Sorry to meet you like this again. I'm a volunteer for Fire District Eight."

She opened a side door of the ambulance and placed the medical bags inside before climbing in the ambulance herself. Once Grandma was loaded into the rig, the other EMTs and Lisa stayed in there for a few more minutes, presumably obtaining vital signs. I sat in my car and made a phone call to my parents in Portland.

My dad said that he and my mother would be on their way as soon as they had packed a bag for the trip northbound.

After a few minutes, Lisa and another volunteer exited the ambulance and it pulled slowly away. I followed a short distance behind. Florescent lights glowed in the back of the ambulance and I could just make out Grandma's defiant figure, sitting up on the gurney, arms crossed, looking displeased. She turned to the paramedic and said something, probably along the lines of "I don't need no damn IV." I fully expected that she would also have some choice words for the driver by the time she arrived at the ER, likely chiding him for the route he took or cursing the many bumps, potholes, and railroad crossings on the way. You were never in any doubt where you stood with Grandma.

The trip to the hospital took about forty minutes. The ambulance had taken its time getting to Mount Vernon. They used no lights or sirens and took a route that I had considered less than optimal. Maybe they were trying to avoid the bumps. Once the ambulance pulled into the ER bay, I drove to the lot north of it and parked my car.

When the driver opened the back doors of the ambulance, Grandma had an IV in her arm and looked defeated, arms at her sides, head down. Her ongoing chatter had ceased, and she seemed to be somewhat doped up, eyelids at half-mast, an oxygen cannula in her nose. Fentanyl was a wonderful drug.

The aid crew wheeled her into the ER and into a very warm room, replete with monitors and an array of medical supplies neatly organized on shelves. I surmised this was the trauma room, or one of them. Grandma was always cold, so 75 degrees was just about right for her. A nurse piled additional warmed blankets on top of her. Another nurse or a technician began taking Grandma's vital signs and attaching her to an EKG machine. The nurses eventually left us alone in the room, allowing Grandma the time to just barely rise above her narcotic-induced stupor, pull the oxygen tube out of her nose and mutter, "Shit."

After what seemed an eternity, a balding, bearded physician with the personality of a potato and the bedside manner of an executioner examined Grandma with great disinterest for about five minutes before the radiology tech whisked her off to X-ray. In the few interactions I had had with this hospital, I wasn't particularly impressed, and today was no exception.

Eventually, the X-ray results came back and it was revealed that Grandma had indeed broken her hip, a femoral neck fracture, to be exact. She would be taken to surgery later in the day where the guys who love power tools would put her back together again. It would be a long recovery, however. Grandma was tough, but no spring chicken, and this would set her back a ways.

As the physician completed the admission paperwork and spoke to the hospitalist in charge of admission, I made my way down to the cafeteria for some coffee and a bite to eat. The food was unpalatable, but the coffee was decent. I leaned back in my chair and watched the parade of human illness pass by, desiccated human hulls procuring nourishment, pushing around their IV pole lifelines, clad in those oh-so-stylish backless gowns. Most thought to wear underwear underneath, a thought for which I was grateful as I attempted to wolf down a meal of unidentifiable meat smashed between two pieces of dried bread.

When I returned, they had Grandma all set up in a room. I sat beside her bed and sipped my lukewarm coffee as chronically irritable nurses flitted in and out of the room, checking Grandma's vital signs and typing in various pieces of information on their bedside computers, their faces illuminated by the glowing screens. There were blood samples to take, additional medical history to gather, and, to Grandma's chagrin and humiliation, a urinary catheter to insert. I stepped out for that part. Just when I thought Grandma was done with the poking and prodding, another nurse or technician stopped by to obtain another blood sample.

Grandma's defeated posture I had noted when she was in the back of the ambulance had been replaced by anger. "I'm so stupid!" she kept muttering to herself.

"Grandma, you're not stupid. These things happen."

"Well they don't happen to me. I've got things to do!"

"Like what, Grandma? Play bingo?"

"Brian, I swear to God…" She balled up her fists and shook her head.

"Oh don't start. You don't even believe in God."

"Maybe not, but I believe in coffee and Marlboro Lights. Can you believe they won't let me smoke?"

"Yes, Grandma. I can believe they won't let you smoke. Do you want to blow yourself to smithereens? You're on oxygen."

"What the hell is a smithereen?"

"Just an expression. Smoking is bad for you."

"No. No it isn't. The smokes haven't killed me yet."

"Well, they nearly did. You're just lucky. Rest, do what the doctors say, and heal up."

Grandma was silent for a minute, then spoke. "Did I tell you how all this happened?"

"You tripped over a dog?"

"Yeah, that little shit, Charlie, the Yorkshire Terror."

"Terrier."

Whatever. He's a terror to me. That hairball with legs is about three pounds of useless. He decided to take himself for a walk and ends up right on my front porch. Well, I hear this yipping so I open the door to see where it's coming from. Turns out he's right in front of the door. So I go ass over teakettle and Charlie runs off, probably to crap on somebody's flower bed. This is why we have the leash rule!"

"I'm sure Dorothy and Art feel terrible about it."

"I certainly hope so. I'll up their lot fees if I don't get an apology in the next couple of days." Grandma grinned, which was rather frightening, considering that her teeth were sitting in a plastic container beside her bed. Unnerving though it was, it was the first time I had seen Grandma crack a smile since she had fallen.

I arose, took a last swig of my coffee, and bid Grandma adieu for the day. I would be back tomorrow to see her after her hip had been repaired.

COMPLICATIONS

My Darth Vader Imperial March ringtone jarred me from my slumber at seven thirty the next morning. It was my father on the other end of the line, absent his usual jovial tone. "Brian, there's been a complication. Your grandmother's had a stroke."

"What?"

"Apparently it happened during the surgery. When she came out of the anesthesia, she couldn't talk and now she can't move her right arm or leg."

"Jesus. Are you at the hospital now?"

"Yes, your mother and I are with her. She's awake but she isn't making much sense."

"Alright, I'll be there as soon as I can get ready."

As I made the long drive back to Skagit Valley Hospital, the same one I had just made the previous day, I began to think about how life can change in an instant. Grandma was old, tough as nails, but still she was in her ninth decade, and I guess I had pushed out of my mind until now how tenuous her hold was on life. Her invincibility had seemed to me without question until now, and the notion that her end might be near was something I hadn't been prepared to face.

I walked into Grandma's room to find my parents holding vigil. Mom had never had an especially close relationship with her mother-in-law, but she was there to support my dad, who held Grandma's hand.

As for Grandma, she appeared to have sunk even further into the bed than she had the last time I saw her. An oxygen cannula snaked into her nose, delivering the air that her scarred lungs could no longer provide. Dad was seated on the side I was told was paralyzed, so I went to her left side and held her hand.

"Grandma, can you hear me?"

She opened her eyes halfway and cast an unfocused gaze in my direction. "Salad," she said, or rather croaked.

"Salad?" I looked across the bed at my father, who looked bemused and shrugged his shoulders. "Are you in any pain, Grandma?"

"Salad."

"That's the only thing she's said since we got here," said my father. "Can you hear me, Mom? Salad. Are they treating you okay? Salad. I don't think she's had a salad in her entire life."

"I sure hope that resolves," I said. "We can't have her sitting at board meetings saying 'salad' the entire time."

My dad didn't see the humor in my last statement. "The doctor said she is likely to improve in the next few days to weeks. Unfortunately, she had her stroke at some point during the surgery, so obviously they couldn't use the clot buster drug to reverse it." Dad scratched his balding head and took a sip of his lukewarm coffee. "But…if anyone can pull out of this, she can. You know your Grandma. She's probably just irritated that she's missing bingo because of this."

"Dad, she doesn't even play bingo."

We both chuckled and fell back into silence. Grandma occasionally reached up with her good hand to scratch her nose. From time to time she would open her eyes and peer around for a few seconds, appear unimpressed, and then fall back into a stupor, snoring loudly.

"Geez," said Dad. Whatever drugs they've given her, I'd like some."

After a while of sitting in silence with Grandma, a stunningly attractive, statuesque black woman walked into the room, squirted a gob of sanitizer on her hands, and then introduced herself. "Hi," she said. "I'm Stella. I'm one of the neurology docs." Her white coat read "Stella Edwards, MD, PhD, Department of Neurology."

Dr. Edwards was friendly and professional but spoke very fast and had a habit of starting each sentence with the word "so."

"So, Mrs. Bowman had a stroke involving the middle cerebral artery, which is, unfortunately, really, really common. It affected her speech center, which is typically on the left side of the brain, as well as her motor function. That's why you're seeing the weakness on the right."

"What are her chances for full recovery?" asked my dad.

"So, the occlusion was fairly distal, which means far downstream in the circulation, and so that is generally predictive of a better outcome than when it's more proximal, or farther upstream, but it's really difficult to project exactly how well she'll do in the long term."

I understood everything Dr. Edwards said, but I doubted my father did. I was the only one in the family with any anatomical or medical training. My father had worked in computer sales his entire working life. Nonetheless, he nodded emphatically at everything Dr. Edwards said. He was always so afraid of disappointing people. I would have to explain things to him later.

Dr. Edwards did an examination on Grandma which included checking her pupils, patellar reflexes, and grips on both sides. She then removed the stethoscope from around her neck, listened to Grandma's lungs, which I didn't expect to sound very healthy, and pushed on her abdomen.

"So not a lot of progress at this point from where we were earlier, but I'm hopeful that she will continue to progress in the coming days and weeks. The good news is that I'm not seeing any new deficits. Her vital signs are all stable, and aside from her COPD, she's fairly healthy. I'm working with Dr. Gupta, the surgeon, to come up with a care plan. So far, we're holding her Coumadin due to bleeding risk after surgery, but she does have atrial fibrillation, so I anticipate talking to the hospitalist about re-establishing that soon. So, any questions?"

My dad and I both shook our heads. When it came to the brain, such a complex and little-understood organ, it was next to impossible to predict how it would react. On Grandma's side, however, was her tenacity and irascibility.

Dr. Edwards smiled, shook hands with all of us, then re-sanitized her hands and walked out with the purpose of one who spends her days going from patient to patient and doing her best to care personally for each one of them. I was impressed with her.

Eventually my parents and I decided to leave and let Grandma get some sleep. I touched her shoulder lightly and said, "Bye Grandma, we'll be back soon."

She opened her eyes wide, looked straight at me and announced "Salad" as though she had never been surer of anything in her life.

THE NEWEST NUDIST

The next morning, I walked a half-mile or so from Grandma's trailer to the pool area, hoping to relax, catch some sun, and maybe take a swim. I had dug out an old pair of shorts from the bottom of my suitcase that I figured would suffice for swim trunks and wore them underneath my ragged sweatpants. Nude and partly nude couples walked by, all of them smiling and saying hello.

As soon as I approached the gate that surrounded the pool, I knew I had a problem. A metal sign below the latch read "Swimwear Prohibited. Nude Swimming Only." This was really a hitch in my plans. As a dedicated "textile" I had no intentions on revealing my pasty white epidermis to everyone at the pool.

I nearly turned on my heel and walked back to the trailer but then decided to check out the pool anyway. I opened the latch and walked into the enclosure. I set down my bag with my towel and book and stood for a moment not really knowing what to do.

After a minute or so of standing there, feeling very out of place, I began to realize that a few people were staring at me. I guess I could understand why. Here I was, bundled up in a long-sleeve T-shirt and sweatpants, gawping like a fool at all the naked people. I doffed my T-shirt, then my sweatpants, feeling confident that I was now appropriately attired in my wrinkled gym shorts and flip-flops. Dammit. They're still staring. So I did what any reasonable person would do; I sat down on a chaise and pretended I was invisible. I took out my "sippy cup" full of ice and gin and began to sip on it gingerly.

I got away with this routine for about five more minutes, enjoying my drink and the sun, until a leathery nude woman approached and advised me that if I was to spend time in the pool area, I must be nude. She was friendly enough about it but had a note of authority in her voice that made me think I should probably do as instructed. I apologized and then decided I had better either leave or "take the plunge."

I stood up, tugged on my waistband, took a deep breath and yanked down my shorts. My heart pounded in my chest as I stood there, shorts around my ankles, naked as the day I was born. I felt breezes in places I had never felt them before. My first reaction, which made no real sense, was that I was committing some kind of public indecency. I half-expected everyone to look at me and I experienced an odd mixture of disappointment and relief when nobody did.

Well, at least for now, I didn't have to worry about what had been my biggest fear of social nudity—a spontaneous erection. In fact, the anxiety of getting naked in public and the ensuing adrenaline rush had the opposite effect on my genitalia, shunting blood to my core and away from my extremities. Everything had shrunken to nearly child-size proportions. I sat. My heart rate began slowly to return to normal. I opened my book, which doubled as a cover-up for my exposed genitals.

After reading for about half an hour, my neck began to ache a bit and my eyes were dry and strained. My sippy cup of gin and tonic that sat on the small table beside me, now more water than alcohol, sweated in the mid-eighties sunshine, such a rarity here but such a welcome one. Perspiration dripped from my armpits and my chest, a sheen of sweat beading up on sunscreen. My penis, now perfused with blood and restored to its former flaccid glory, lolled onto my right thigh; my scrotum, fully slackened in the hot sunshine, glistened with sweat. I even moved my book from my lap and set it aside. Oddly, after a while seated by the pool, genitals exposed to all comers, I no longer felt naked in the company of so many other unclothed folks. Soon, there was no breeze either, and since the heat was pretty much evenly distributed over all of my body, it was difficult to feel that one particular area, usually covered by a pair of swim trunks, was any different than the rest.

It was almost time for a refill on my drink. The pool looked so refreshing, as did the shower beside it. Each visitor showered in either a luxurious or a perfunctory manner, an almost spiritual cleansing in which sunscreen and residual sweat were washed away, before plunging into the pool.

The cross-section of humanity was on display today. Two elderly couples, probably in their late seventies or early eighties, lay on chaises poolside. Occasionally one of them would, very slowly and accompanied by groans, rise from their seats and incrementally descend into the shallow end of the pool. Children squealed and ran along the pool edge, dodging older nudists and periodically being scolded by an old-timer reminding them not to run.

As I was about to arise and refill my drink, I spotted a slim figure coming through the gate. She wore a flowing multicolored summer dress and pink flip-flops. Her eyes were hidden by huge sunglasses and she wore a floppy black sun hat. Perhaps I'd wait a minute.

The woman made her way around to my side of the pool and set her bag down on a nearby chaise, leaving one empty between the two of us. She doffed her hat and shook out long blond hair that had been done up in a braid. Then, without the slightest hesitation, she slipped her dress over her head. She was naked underneath.

I watched with great interest as the dress slipped past her muscular thighs, brushing her lush, thick, brown pubic hair, up her torso to her perfect, pert breasts and supple neck, adorned with a gold cross on a chain. She stuffed the dress into her bag and began laying out her towel. In addition to being completely naked, she was tanned from head to toe and breathtakingly gorgeous. Her toenails were adorned with pink polish. On her left second toe she wore a silver toe ring. Her thighs and calves were thick and toned. Beneath her mons, I caught just a slight glimpse of her labia, mostly covered by hair and a glint of a labial piercing. Silver? Her belly wasn't flat, but just slightly, pleasingly rounded. She was by no means overweight, but she wasn't a stick either.

I felt my penis begin to subtly shift position and then I became, momentarily, completely aware of my own nudity. I panicked as blood began to flow into my nether regions. The last thing I needed was an unwanted erection in front of not only this beautiful woman, but also the residents and visitors of Deep Valley. I grabbed my book, sitting beside me on the table, and hastily covered my groin.

The beauty settled onto her towel and sighed quietly, chest out and legs slightly parted. She seemed 100% at home in her body. Then she turned toward me, pushing her sunglasses slightly down onto her nose.

"Brian?"

"Oh…hi!"

"It's Lisa! From the front office?"

"Oh! Hi Lisa!" I was one smooth cat. Had all the best lines.

"How's your grandmother?"

"Hanging in there. It'll be a long rehab for her but she's tough as nails."

"I bet! She's a character. I feel so bad for her and so do Dorothy and Art." Lisa smiled and pushed her sunglasses back up on her nose.

"It's not her first brush with death or serious illness. I think she'll pull through."

"I'm sure she will. I think that woman is immortal."

My mind raced as I attempted to make conversation. Small talk had never been my strong suit. I was always so deathly afraid of making the other person bored that I often engaged in the most banal small talk that later, upon reflection, caused me deep embarrassment.

"So. Getting some sun today?" I asked. As I mentioned, I am pretty smooth with the lines.

Lisa laughed. "Every day. It's probably not good for me, but I slather on the sunscreen before I leave my place. I'd like to think I'm delaying an inevitable case of malignant melanoma."

"I haven't had much sun this year."

"Well, I can see you've had some, cottontail."

I gave Lisa a quizzical look and then realized what defined me from all the other sun worshippers here. I had a clear demarcation at the waist where my shorts normally covered. I had one white ass. I was indeed a cottontail.

"Sorry." Lisa laughed. "I'm just giving you shit. Cottontail is our term for a new nudist with tan lines."

"Oh. Yeah, I guess I have to work on that." Prior to my move to the park, I had spent many a late afternoon sunning on my deck, shirtless and wearing shorts and boots.

"At least you remembered your towel," said Lisa.

I was beginning to assemble a rudimentary set of nudist rules in my head, not in any particular order: 1. Remember your towel; 2. No photography without permission; 3. No swimsuits in or around the swimming pool; 4. Never stare and always look your fellow nudists in the eye. I may have been failing on that last one. Thank goodness for dark sunglasses. This woman was gorgeous.

I had remembered my towel, victory #1, and, victory #2, my genitals had behaved themselves, at least for now. My biggest fear, that I would become visibly aroused in the presence of a nude woman, was temporarily allayed. I was so confident, in fact, that I removed my book from my lap and placed it on the table that supported my drink.

Lisa's glance quickly but subtly focused on my groin, no more than a second, and then she re-focused on my face. "I could use a drink," she said.

Now she was speaking my language. "What is your drink of choice?"

"I'm a cranberry and vodka kind of a girl. You?"

"Gin and tonic."

"Oh my. How sophisticated!"

"Always."

"Shall we?"

The bar was just a short walk from the pool, out of the enclosure and around the corner. Bare Spirits, in the tradition of so many Northwest nudist establishments, was open only on the weekends. Lisa arose first and as I followed her I noted that the view from the rear was equally as pleasing as the one from the front. Her skin was flawless, her buttocks firm and round.

The proprietor of the bar/snack bar/convenience store was an elderly gent who appeared to have been managing the establishment since the beginning of time. A weathered and wizened man of nearly eighty, the legend known as Mr. Dan hunched on a stool behind an open laptop computer. The glow from the laptop accentuated every wrinkle on his face.

He smiled as Lisa and I walked in through the open glass door.

"Hey there, Lisa!" he called. "How are you, gorgeous?"

Lisa didn't mind the old men flirting with her. Besides being flattering, for her there seemed a precipitous drop-off in the creepiness factor for men north of sixty-five years old. After that age, they were harmless, she thought, just trying to somehow re-engage with their youth, even if for only a few moments.

"Mr. Dan, you're back!"

"Yeah, I'm too cantankerous to die." He chuckled and hacked at the same time. "Got out of the hospital a week ago."

"What happened to you?" Lisa asked.

"A touch of pneumonia and I might have had a minor stroke, but I'm hanging in there. Who's your friend"?"

"Dan, this is Brian. Brian, Dan. He was the first president of Deep Valley and for some reason, he still won't leave."

Dan laughed and seemed as though he might choke on the ill-fitting dentures that had been clacking around in this mouth since before Brian and Lisa had arrived. Dan extended a withered hand.

I noticed what appeared to be a pacemaker protruding under the thin skin on the left side of his chest. "Nice to meet you, Brian." His gaze darted between Lisa and me. "You be careful of this one, Brian."

I met his gaze with a slightly quizzical look. I smiled. "Okay, will do."

"I mean…" began Dan again. "Be careful with this one. She's like a daughter to me."

"More like granddaughter," said Lisa. "The granddaughter you never wanted to have."

"You got that right, darling. What can I do you for?"

"I'll have a cranberry and vodka," said Lisa.

"Gin and tonic for me," I chimed in.

"Solid choices, my friends. Gorgeous day, ain't it?"

"Sure is," said Lisa. "Getting my tan on."

Dan poured our drinks with a quavering hand and set them on the bar. "Six dollars," he said. "I'll only charge you for the one. Welcome to Deep Valley, Brian."

"Ah, thanks, Dan," said Lisa. "You can just put it on my account."

"Done," said Dan.

Lisa and I walked back out to the pool, drinks in hand, wearing nothing, clothed only in sunshine. It seemed so surreal. A few days prior, I had been experiencing a mid-life upheaval, leaving my wife and my career, with no particular direction in life, yet here I was, living in a dream, if only for a while. My penis swung freely to and fro and I hoped, naively, that nobody noticed I was once again semi-turgid.

Lisa and I settled back into our lounge chairs, sipped on our drinks, and gazed at the pool. An older couple came into the pool area with two small children in tow, one of whom waddled by wearing a dragon floaty and goggles. The older woman was quite large and walked with a cane, while the man was thin and hairy. They could have been parents but were more likely grandparents, I surmised. A gray-haired woman walked by, a towel slung over her shoulder. When she removed the towel and sat down nearby, I realized that she was missing a breast. Nobody batted an eye. A man greeted her warmly with a "nudist hug," accentuated by a hand clap on the back, their respective hips farther back than they would be in a textile environment. I never imagined that there could be such a place in which everyone was free to be themselves, scars, warts, cellulite, and all. When I had come here as a kid, I had never noticed. As I approached middle age, though, this fact was decidedly refreshing.

Lisa turned from her back to her side, facing me and sliding her sunglasses on top of her head. "So what made you take the plunge and become a nudist?"

"Well, I'm not really a nudist. It's just that I felt like lying out by the pool and possibly taking a dip. The pool looked so inviting, but there's this sign here about no swimming suits. I figured now was as good a time as any to expose myself to nature. I've actually never been naked in public before."

"Ah. Gotcha. What do you think so far?"

"Nice, for the most part. It's taking a bit of getting used to seeing older folks naked." I thought for a moment. "Actually, it's taking a bit of getting used to seeing myself naked!"

Lisa laughed. "I don't think you have anything to worry about, Brian. So, you live with your grandmother?"

"Yeah, it's...it's a bit of a long story."

"I won't pry," Lisa said but I could just tell she wanted to. I had a pretty good idea this gal was smart enough to figure out that if a guy in his thirties goes to live with his grandmother in her trailer at a nudist resort, his life is not exactly going swimmingly.

"It's okay. It's just kind of…where I've landed for the moment."

Lisa nodded and took a sip of her drink. She was silent for a minute, then said, "Hey, you want to take a swim?"

We took turns rinsing the sweat and sunscreen off ourselves in the rather weak, shockingly cool shower and then plunged into the pool. Well, Lisa plunged. I stepped into the shallow end, slowly acclimating myself to the water. It was the story of my life, really, caution and risk aversion. Lisa swam laps like a pro, dodging excited children while I waded to chest height and stood with my arms folded like some sort of timid pool referee.

Lisa emerged from the water like a mermaid, blond locks matted down, pool water dripping from her small breasts. "Hey, you ever swam in Lake Haussmann?" she asked.

"I haven't," I replied.

"You really should. It's so refreshing. I like to run a couple of miles before I swim. Really gets the blood pumping. Hey! You want to join me some time?"

"Sure," I said, and I'm sure it didn't sound very sincere. I had the athletic ability of a blobfish, and I wasn't sure if I could keep up with her.

"Great!" Lisa swam a couple more laps, then got out via a ladder on the deep end. She squeezed the excess water out of her hair and then walked back towards her chair. I followed suit. We air dried on our towels, warmed by the sun, sipping our drinks.

"Got any plans for the rest of the day?" asked Lisa.

"Yeah, I need to go to the hospital to see my grandma. You?"

"You're looking at it!" Lisa reclined her chair fully and flipped over to her stomach. "Evening out my tan!"

I looked at my phone and realized I'd been at the pool nearly three hours, much longer than I had expected. It was time to pack up and head back to the trailer.

"Nice meeting you, again," I said, as I stood and stuffed my belongings into my bag. "Maybe I'll take you up on that swim and run." I was dubious about keeping up with her, but I certainly wanted to see her again.

"Wednesday?"

"That will work. What time?"

"I've got all day."

"Meet you at four here?"

"It's a deal."

I donned my sexy ensemble of old gym shorts, sweatpants, and a baggy T-shirt and trudged back to the trailer, a bit light-headed and in need of water. I was already behind schedule to see Grandma.

Visiting Grandma

If I was going to visit my ailing grandmother in the hospital, the least I could do was to look somewhat presentable for her. I took a real shower, with soap and shampoo, and then put on a pair of nicely pressed slacks and a button-up shirt. Prior to Grandma's untimely departure from the park, she had kindly ironed my clothes and placed them neatly at the end of my bed, for which I was grateful. This time, she hadn't balled them up.

I felt a bit giddy as I drove westward, savoring my recent encounter with the lovely Lisa, firefighter/EMT and nudist extraordinaire. I didn't even know her last name. Not only was she pleasing to the eye, she seemed to be intelligent as well, which was my biggest turn-on. After a few minutes of fantasizing, my left brain reminded my right that I was still, technically, married and admonished it for thinking of women when I should be concentrating on the road in front of me. I had never been too successful at shutting off my left cerebral cortex.

As I reached the hospital parking lot some forty minutes and countless daydreams later, I was unable to find a parking space to save my life and spent ten minutes circumnavigating the lot in great vexation before I spotted an elderly woman attempting to extricate her yacht-sized Cadillac out of a too-small parking space.

After she had finally completed an eighteen-point turn and slowly drove off, I seized the opportunity and darted into her space. I shut off the engine, parked, and then walked through the sliding glass doors that led to the hospital. I stopped at the gift shop to pick up some red roses for Grandma before heading up.

When I reached Grandma's room, I was heartened when she looked at me and smiled, an asymmetrical smile, but a genuine one nevertheless. Mom and Dad were again at her side and they got up to greet me and give me a hug as I walked in. Grandma's younger sister Maxine was there as well. She was a weary-looking woman who never smoked or drank but somehow, despite her ostensibly healthy lifestyle, managed to look significantly older than her sister. She wore a Rite Aid cashier's vest flecked with cat fur and had multicolored reading glasses on a chain around her neck. Maxine and Grandma were never close, even though they lived within twenty miles of each other. I had never seen Maxine smile, and I figured today would not be the day she would break character.

Grandma continued to grin and said something like, "The cat."

I looked at her quizzically. "What did you say?"

"The cat. The cat!" She waved her good arm around in frustration.

"I'm sorry, Grandma," I said. "I know that you know what you want to say, but you can't get it out."

"Ugh," said Grandma. She sighed and tried again. "The cat. Drag the cat!"

"Oh!" said Dad, as a look of recognition crossed his face. "She's saying 'look what the cat dragged in.' She always used to say that."

Grandma nodded emphatically, sighed, and rolled her eyes. Everyone laughed, even my mother, who was usually very quiet and reserved. It was a much-needed moment of levity in the context of Grandma's very serious health challenges.

"She's saying a few more words today," said Dad. "She even told me I need a haircut. Can you believe that? I think her brain is rewiring itself. Even Dr. Edwards was surprised at how quickly she's progressing. She had physical therapy this morning and she will every morning from here on out. She's getting some movement back in that arm and leg, but she's still a long ways from being able to stand on her own. Depending on how her progress goes, we'll be meeting with a discharge planner in the next few days to discuss moving her to a nursing home."

"Bullshit," said Grandma.

"Sorry, Mom. Rehab facility. Only for a little while, until you get back on your feet." Dad patted her shoulder. Grandma looked annoyed at Dad's patronizing tone. The last thing she wanted was to lose her independence.

"So, Brian," said Dad. "How's life at the nudist colony?" He smirked.

"Not too bad. Also, I've been informed that the proper term is 'Nudist Park'. Ants live in colonies; people don't."

"Humph," said Dad. "I didn't realize nudists had become all politically correct like the rest of this country. You're not participating, are you?"

"Oh, no," I lied. "Who wants to see me without clothes?" I gave my best look of self-referential disgust.

I stayed a bit longer, chatting with my parents and feeling bad that I couldn't include Grandma in the conversation, but she appeared bored with it all and drifted off to sleep eventually. Maxine muttered something about having to go to work, the first words she had spoken since I had arrived. The conversation between my parents and me eventually ebbed and I took this as my cue to exit and head back home.

DALE'S NEW FIELD GLASSES

The Reverend Dale Parkhurst had just arrived home after having finished a marathon Sunday sermon on sexual immorality and immodest dress. It was a favorite subject of his, as evidenced by the fact that four of his last six sermons focused on these topics. Another favorite was Hellfire and the Lord's wrath. Often he combined several of his pet topics into an epic soliloquy, bringing in elements of current culture, such as Gay Pride parades, rap music, and fornication with loose women. At times he would invent evils that didn't actually exist, just so that he could rail against them, such as drive-through abortion clinics. He would turn beet-red and spittle would fly from his mouth as he ranted. His most ardent followers considered him a modern-day prophet.

After throwing his car keys on the kitchen counter and half-heartedly attempting his weekly crossword puzzle without much success, he set down his newspaper and took up his new binoculars. He was going to see what those nudists were up to today.

Dale was immensely pleased with his decision to purchase a high-quality pair of Nikon binoculars that would allow him to closely observe the nudists from his front window. Whereas before it was difficult to even determine their gender from afar, now

Dale had a front-row seat to the den of iniquity masquerading as a Garden of Eden.

Jan Parkhurst sat at the kitchen table and regarded her husband with bemusement. "Well, seen anything interesting, Dale? Do they frolic about? Or is it more like cavorting?"

"They aren't wildlife, dear."

"I just don't understand why you complain so much about having to see naked people, and then make a special effort to see them up close."

"Well, Jan, I'm attempting to confirm that they're up to no good."

"And that involves being able to determine their eye color from a mile away?"

Dale put down his binoculars. He was clearly not getting through to his wife. So thick-headed she was. There was simply nothing normal or Godly about these people showing off their skins in mixed company.

"Did you see it's for sale?" asked Jan.

"What? The nudie park?"

"A woman in my prayer group knows someone who knows someone who says the nudist colony isn't making it and needs to sell. Apparently membership is way down and things are going unrepaired because they don't have the money to fix things."

"Can't say I feel a bit sorry for them," said Dale. "That's God's way of telling those heathens down there to put on some clothes and go back to church."

"Your church?"

"Our church, Jan. You're just as important as I am there. Anyway, why are people in your group associating with known nudists?"

"It's been here in the county for decades, extending its tentacles into the community. You never know when one of your friends or a friend of a friend might be a nudist."

"Humph," said Dale. "Certainly not any of my friends."

"They could be anywhere, living among us as seemingly normal people, wearing clothes, going to work—undercover nudists, Dale! You don't suppose…Dr. Cohen?"

"My dentist?"

"Well, he's a Democrat, so he's probably a nudist as well."

"You may be right," said Dale.

"And those hand gestures? He's probably a homosexual too," said Jan.

"Honestly, Jan." Dale was beginning to get the creeping suspicion that his wife was messing with him. It always took him a while to catch on, and it didn't help that his sense of humor was next to nonexistent. It bothered Dale that his wife was quite a bitter smarter than he.

Jan laughed and playfully smacked her husband's arm. He managed a half-hearted smirk and then went back to his crossword. If it weren't for the fact that she was a preacher's wife, Jan figured she might actually join those heathens at Deep Valley Nudist Resort some time. She might even frolic or cavort.

Dale chewed on his pencil and stared at the wall. "Jan, what's a four-letter word for someone who is overly concerned with decorum or propriety? Starts with p-r."

PRESIDENT BRIAN?

The morning after I visited Grandma, at a very indecent hour for a non-morning person, before I had to opportunity to bathe my brain in caffeine, I awoke to a sharp rapping on my door. I rolled out of bed and swerved in the general direction of the front door.

I opened the door to find Security Bob standing on the porch, wearing his trademark green Bermuda shorts and orange Crocs. "Ya got a minute?" he asked.

"Ummm, okay?"

"Gotta talk to you about your grandma. Come on. I'll give you a ride to the office."

I put on some slippers and trudged behind Security Bob to his golf cart. He drove a short distance to the office, parked the cart, and we walked in. He pointed out a small room adjoining the main office area and indicated for me to take a seat.

Behind the desk was quite possibly the largest nudist I had ever seen in my life, though my experience was, of course, limited. He wore a snow-white beard that extended down to the middle of his expansive chest and peered at me through small round glasses perched at the end of his nose. His hair, or what was left of it, hung in whitish-gray strands over his shoulders. A nudist Santa Claus, all he was missing was the red-and-white outfit. With apparent great difficulty, he stood, groaning as he did so. Though he was completely naked, his genitals were hidden under an apron of abdominal fat. I recognized him as Gunter Kohl, the elected secretary of Deep Valley Nudist Club.

"Hi, I'm Gunter," he said, and extended a meaty hand.

"Brian." I shook his hand.

"You are the professor, yes?" he asked, with a thick German accent.

"I am, yes, or was."

Bob took a seat next to Gunter and took a sip of coffee from a stainless steel mug.

"I was a doctor in Germany, you know. But we need to discuss this matter of your grandmother. As you know, she is the president of the club and currently incapacitated, so for the foreseeable future, we don't have a president." Gunter took a deep breath. "Under the current club bylaws, written many years ago by Bob's father, leadership doesn't go to the vice president or the secretary. It goes to the nearest available relative of the president." He paused. "That would be you, Brian."

I swallowed. "You want me to run this club?"

Gunter and Bob looked at each other and nodded in unison. "Yes, that's basically what we're saying."

"Well, what are my responsibilities?"

Gunter replied, "You would preside over all the meetings, deal with any conflicts that come up, approve new members, and okay any policy changes."

"Why wouldn't the vice president take over? Isn't that kind of the role of the vice president?"

Bob interjected, "It's just not the way the rules were written. Also, Judy's health isn't very good either. I just think she likes the title of Vice President."

"Do I have time to think about it?"

"You do," replied Gunter. "But we'd like an answer maybe, say, in the next week. We have a lot of events coming up."

"And we think you would be great for the position," added Bob.

I couldn't really imagine why these two men would think me of me as a suitable president, even in the interim. I wasn't a nudist and had been here on the grounds for all of five minutes. I was, however, under seventy years of age, and had my health on my side, which ruled out many of the long-term members of the club.

"If you decide to do it," said Gunter, "you'll need to come to the next club meeting a week on Saturday and we'll do a special election."

"Okay. I'll think about it. This is, I take it, a volunteer position?"

Gunter chuckled. "A labor of love, son. We'll make you a nudist yet!"

I wasn't so sure about that.

Bob and Gunter both rose to shake my hand, indicating that the short meeting was concluded. We shook and I promised once again to consider the proposal. As I turned to leave, Bob said, "Oh, and one more thing…"

"Yes?"

"If you can, try to make it to our wine and cheese party tomorrow night. We usually sit around the fire for a while and then, depending on the crowd, somebody might even fire up the karaoke machine. It would be a great opportunity for you to meet some of the other members."

"I'll be there!"

THE FIRE PIT

.

The following evening I made my way to the fire pit. The fire was just in its incipient phase, gathering strength, as an older woman periodically stoked it and threw on more firewood from a large nearby woodpile. As she prodded the fire with what appeared to be the charred remains of a rake, the dry wood, seasoned over months, popped and spewed embers here and there, dangerously close to her large, dangling, unrestrained breasts. I recognized her as Dolores, the woman I had seen gardening a few days prior. Several members relaxed in chairs fireside, some nude, some clothed, and some partially clothed, periodically scooting their chairs farther back as the fire grew under the patient coaxing of Dolores, the Tender of Flames.

Near the fire pit was a folding table on which was laid a variety of snack trays, including the obligatory cheese and crackers, shrimp with dip, and two or three plates of cookies. Several wine containers, both boxed and bottled, sat at the other end of the table. My contribution was brownies and since I am such a terrible baker, they came from the local grocery store.

After placing my offering on the table, I pulled a chair up to the fire and sat. I experienced a few awkward moments while I surveyed the crowd and tried to figure out if or how to interact.

Everyone seemed to know each other well and were talking and laughing amongst themselves. In addition to Dolores, I recognized the very old man I had seen walking around the lake the other day and his somewhat younger companion. He leaned forward, balancing his hands on an ornately carved cane, and stared into the flames. He smiled slightly as I made eye contact with him and then went back to his flame watching. To his right sat a middle-aged man with a beard so long it extended to his groin. His body was turned to the right, legs crossed, and he appeared to be having a very animated conversation with two nude women, one of whom had dyed pink hair. The other wore her hair in a gray crew cut.

Dolores, now apparently satisfied with her fire, laid down her charred stoker, turned, and slowly lowered herself into a towel-covered chair immediately to my left. "Oof!" she said. "My back. I need a rest after that." Everyone chuckled in recognition of the challenges of getting old. The fire blazed. It was starting to get quite warm where I was sitting.

Dolores breathed heavily for a minute and then turned towards me, extending a hand. "I'm Dolores."

"Brian."

"Clara's grandson?"

"Yep."

"I was so sorry to hear about her accident."

"Thanks. It's a tough one for her, but she's getting better every day."

"Oh, I know," said Dolores. "She's nearly indestructible. I've known her for eight years. She was one of the first people I met when I moved up here."

"You live up here full time?" I asked.

"I travel a bit here and there but yes, it's been my home base since I sold my house in Mukilteo in 2012." She took a swig of wine from a red plastic Solo cup she had balanced on the edge of her chair. "This place is my little piece of paradise." She grinned broadly. "And I don't even have to put on clothes to chat with my neighbors."

"Sounds great!" I said. "So how did you decide to live up here full time?"

"My husband died eight years ago. Sam was a good provider and a decent man, but he could also be somewhat of a control freak. We never went on vacations, never even so much as a weekend camping trip. He kept the budget very tight. We never had children, which I regret, so we didn't have to pay for college, of course. Even when I would get together with my friends, he would call me constantly, wondering when I'd be home. Well, after Sam died, I decided I didn't want to spend my golden years in an empty house, staring out the window, wasting what little time I had left feeling lonesome and sorry for myself."

Dolores took the last sip of her wine and then looked disappointedly at the empty cup, as if she was expecting a refill to well up from the bottom.

"So anyway," she continued, "an open-minded friend of mine introduced me to Deep Valley Nudist Park. First time I came up here, I took off all my clothes in the first ten minutes. It was exhilarating. Guess I was ready to become a nudist! I was seventy years old and fifty pounds overweight, and nobody cared that I didn't look like a model. Everyone was so welcoming, looked me in the eye, they didn't stare at my lopsided boobs or my knee replacement scars. People just accepted me for who I am. I knew

I was home. About six months later, I put my house up for sale and I've been a full-time resident ever since."

Dolores adjusted herself in her seat and then stooped down to re-tie her tennis shoes, the only item of clothing she wore. "Well, I'm going for a refill. Would you like anything? I brought some decent Cabernet, if you'd like."

Having observed the effort that it took the elderly Dolores to sit as well as tie her shoes, I decided it best if I offered to refill her glass myself. "I've got it," I said, and took her Solo cup from her.

"You sure? Very nice of you."

I refilled her cup and got one for myself, grabbing some cheese and crackers along the way. Numerous other people dribbled in, grabbing chairs from a nearby stack, and expanded the circle. Nobody seemed to go long without speaking or being spoken to. Soon the air was full of good-natured chatter, accompanied by the crackling of the fire. I handed Dolores her Solo cup and sat.

"Cheers to life," she said, and clinked her cup against mine. "You see all these people?" Dolores swept her arm, indicating the gathering crowd of nudists happily toasting themselves, the sun going down, the shadows beginning to form. "Can you tell what any of these people do for a living? Who is rich? Who is poor?"

I shook my head.

"I had a very comfortable life for over forty-five years. Sam was very successful in business and we lived in luxury. Doesn't matter now. Dave over there"—she turned her head to the side, indicating the man with the massive beard—"is a watercolorist and couldn't care less about money, lives in a yurt on the back part of the property. Those two ladies he's talking to, Carol and her partner Sue? Well, they're both doctors. I think Carol's an interventional cardiologist. But who can tell? Carol is also the only lesbian

Republican I've ever met!" Dolores laughed. "I'll tell you a story about her. We had a member collapse up here a few years back and Carol started CPR, kept it up until the medics got here. She wasn't wearing anything but a pair of shorts and flip-flops, dripping sweat and all."

"What was the outcome?" I asked.

"See that guy standing over there?" She pointed at a very thin, very tan man standing and talking with another member. I recognized him as Mr. Dan the bartender. "Ever notice his pacemaker?"

"Wow, that's awesome."

"Anyway," Dolores continued, "without clothes, nobody knows your social status and everyone's on an even playing field. Forget politics or money. I happen to know that Carol and Sue are well-off but they never talk about it. Carol won't tell you she's a doctor unless you ask her what she does. She drives an old Toyota Camry when she could drive a Ferrari. We all just bond over our love of being naked.

"In fact, I've often thought that our bodies are kind of like vehicles that we just get to drive through life to get us around. We've had some Dodge Ram Power Diesels come through here, an occasional Maserati, and more than our share of mini-vans, but most of us are like Toyota Camrys—solid and dependable, but not very striking to look at. We all just bond over our love of being naked and free the way we were intended to be."

"I never thought of it that way. And without pants, where would you put your wallet anyway?"

Dolores laughed. She touched my arm briefly with a rather sweaty hand. "So, Brian. How did you come to be a nudist?"

"Well, I'm not really sure that I am," I said, then thought better of it. If I was to take a leadership role in this club, I had better represent myself as one of them. "Actually, I'm learning to be a nudist. I'm acclimating. Kind of a Nudist-in-Training."

"Nudist-in-Training. NIT! I like that!" said Dolores.

"I'm here temporarily, but while my grandmother recovers, I may be taking over some of her duties."

"Great. Well, anything I can do to help, just ask me. I've been here a while and I know how things work."

"Thanks, Dolores. I'm hoping Grandma gets back on her feet quickly."

"Such a dear lady. I was sorry to hear of her fall."

"Thanks. She's a tough one, though."

Dolores left to grab some cookies and then started a conversation with a friend of hers she had met at the snack table. I settled back and sipped my wine as happy naked people chatted around me. At some point, when it had become completely dark and some people dressed or put on bathrobes, the party adjourned to inside the clubhouse for karaoke.

As it turned out, naked karaoke was just as painful on the ears as clothed karaoke, but everyone seemed to have a great time. Just as it didn't matter if nobody had a perfect body, it also didn't matter if nobody could sing particularly well. The only exception was Dave, the yurt-dwelling, bearded hippie, who sang a particularly accurate version of John Lennon's "Imagine." At the end of it, everyone cheered and a few gave high-fives as he triumphantly walked back down the aisle to his seat, grinning from ear to ear. I made a mental note to introduce myself to him at some point as he was one of the few young people I had encountered at Deep Valley, and by young I meant under fifty.

The karaoke continued well into the night with people leaving and others showing up. Another very old man who leaned on a cane and had a penis like a truncheon and a scrotum that was nearly a trip hazard snuck in around ten o'clock at night and stood in the back, drinking coffee from a canteen. Eventually he got up on stage and sang Elvis Presley's "Suspicious Minds" in a remarkably baritone voice.

I missed Grandma, even if her version of "Son of a Preacher Man" was both screechy and dreadfully off-key. I wondered if she would ever recover enough to get behind the microphone again, let alone stand unassisted. Aging was a bitch, though Grandma hadn't done herself any favors by smoking two packs of cigarettes a day for sixty years and drinking what probably amounted to an Olympic-sized swimming pool full of gin in her lifetime. It was remarkable that she was alive after it all. She'd virtually embalmed herself from the inside out. I sipped my drink and watched, so much the observer rather than the participant. I reminded myself that I needed to get involved in the club's events or I would forever be an outsider in a place that was to be my home for the foreseeable future. Sometime soon, I told myself, I would get up and sing, albeit badly. I just hoped that the members would forgive me for the assault on their ears. What would I sing? What could I sing? The only one song I could think of off-hand that wouldn't cause everyone's ears to bleed spontaneously was "Puttin' on the Ritz" by Taco. It seemed to fit my naturally monotone voice.

As the evening wound down and people began to disperse, I decided it was time to take my leave and head back to Grandma's trailer. I hadn't worked up the courage to sing yet. Maybe next time. I bid goodbye to Dolores, who hadn't participated either. I think she just liked to visit with friends and drink her wine, which kind of made her a kindred soul.

As I made my way back to Grandma's trailer, I reflected on the evening. The concept of naked karaoke made me giggle a bit. It was just so silly. On the wall at the clubhouse, I had seen an advertisement for Bare Bowling sponsored by a club in Oregon. Presumably this meant that a bunch of folks wearing nothing but bowling shoes would descend on a local bowling alley and "bowl in the buff." It was really the silliness of these events that made them compelling, I thought. Sure, there were aspects to nudism that were serious, such as body confidence, but nudism seemed a way of life that didn't take itself too seriously, and that was refreshing.

Feeling the buzz from a bottle's worth of red wine, I sat in the silence and darkness on my bed for a few moments. The campfire had been a pleasant way to draw folks together in conversation on a cool Northwest night, but it sure stunk. My hair and clothing were infused with the smell of fire and I hated to go to bed feeling dirty. I showered, toweled off, and then got into bed. I didn't bother to don my customary nightwear—tighty-whities and a T-shirt. The odd thing was that, prior to the last few weeks, I had never even questioned why I bothered to wear anything at all to bed. It was just what I had always worn what my dad had worn to bed, and maybe even his father before him. Other than keeping the chill off, I wondered if it served a purpose. It was always pretty warm in Grandma's trailer. Even in her absence, I kept the fire stoked, but damped down to a reasonable level, a sentinel waiting for Grandma's return. As I rolled over and adjusted my trio of pillows, I relished the feel of the sheets on my back and bare buttocks. No T-shirt to bind up as I rolled. My genitals were free to find their own position of comfort according to gravity, unbound by redundant fabric. There was no part of my body that was too cool or too hot and I fell to sleep quickly, sprawled half on my side, arms and legs off at weird angles, like a squashed bug.

JAN'S ADVENTURE

Jan Parkhurst awoke promptly to her alarm at 8 a.m. She reached her left hand out to where her husband would normally lie, but then realized he was already on the road, probably at the first of several pastoral care appointments during which he would visit the sick and the dying as part of his Saturday duties as pastor. On most of these occasions, Jan would accompany him, riding shotgun in his elderly Cadillac, offering a reassuring smile and a warm hand to the shut-ins and the moribund among Rev. Parkhurst's ever-growing flock.

Last night, however, she had informed her husband that she was going to meet her long-time friend Rosemary, a ponderous woman who suffered from gout and hypertension. It had been too long since their last meeting, Rosemary needed the company, and who knows how long she would be around? Surely Dale wouldn't object to Jan forgoing her wifely pastoral duties to visit a homebound friend of forty years?

Predictably, Dale had objected, stating that he would be glad to include Rosemary in his pastoral rounds. After all, Rosemary had been a parishioner for many years, and a reliable contributor to the church's coffers.

Jan had made up a story about how Rosemary had converted to atheism and thus was no longer interested in the blessings of Jesus Christ. Dale had huffed and gone to bed ambivalent and a bit miffed.

Slightly giddy with her unexpected freedom and the prospect of an exciting day ahead, Jan bolted out of bed with an ebullience and energy that belied her fifty-nine years. Today was the day she would fulfill her dream—taboo in the eyes of her husband—to visit a nudist resort.

Still clad in her modest, ankle-length nightgown, she brushed her teeth with vigor and gulped down her pills for low thyroid. Today was not the day to feel old.

Jan stood in front of her full-length mirror and contemplated herself for a minute. She studied her wrinkles and fine lines, her graying hair, and her sagging skin. Then, with a flourish, she pulled her nightgown over her head and cast it on the floor. There she stood, naked as the day she was born.

She contemplated the effects of gravity on her breasts and belly, her hysterectomy scar, the varicose veins that affected her right leg more than the left, and her dense, untamed patch of pubic hair. She had shaved it all off five years ago out of boredom and in a vain attempt to put some spark back into her relationship with Dale. It had backfired. She thought the word he had used was "Trollope."

Am I still beautiful? Do I resemble in any way the woman my husband married thirty years ago?

Jan put the thought out of her head for the time being and proceeded to get dressed for the day: underwear, jeans that she felt were way too small, a bra, and shapeless flowered sweatshirt. She scurried to the door and donned her pink tennis shoes.

She climbed into her maroon 1996 Ford Windstar, old and reliable like she was, and turned the key in the ignition. Today was going to be a big day.

On her drive, Jan's thoughts were a complex mixture of excitement, foreboding, titillation, and not just a little bit of guilt. Only a few puffy clouds could be seen through her sunroof. She donned her sunglasses to avoid the glare.

She pulled up to Deep Valley's massive locked gate. Butterflies danced in her stomach. Or perhaps it was diarrhea? She hoped not. I mean, of all times. With slightly tremulous fingers, she punched in the gate code that Gunter had given her the previous day. With a clank and a whir, the gate began to open. Jan got back in her van and drove up to the office.

Gunter had seen Jan pull up, and he was waiting, leaning on the counter, wearing an open plaid button-up flannel shirt and a pair of checkered pajama bottoms. He was nothing if not stylish.

Jan walked through the front door with all the confidence of a gazelle approaching a grizzly Bear. Gunter smiled warmly. Jan's shoulder's relaxed slightly.

"Here for the day?" asked Gunter.

"Maybe an hour or so," replied Jan timidly.

"Have you been here before?" asked Gunter.

"Never."

"The day fee is fifteen dollars," said Gunter. "You can pay by cash, check, or card and I'll give you a slip to put under the windshield of your car so everyone knows you've registered."

Jan, who hadn't quite moved into the era of plastic, retrieved her checkbook from the cavernous abyss of the giant purse she carried. Laboriously and in flawless handwriting, she wrote out a check to Deep Valley Nudist Resort. Even just writing the words made her feel a bit naughty.

Gunter slid a single piece of paper across the counter. "Here's a map of the grounds. Feel free to explore. The only place nudity is required is in and around the pool area. Remember your towel and have fun!"

With the yellow carbon copy of her registration in hand, Jan walked back to her car. She glanced at the map that Gunter had provided and drove towards the clubhouse. It occurred to her that she hadn't quite figured out yet what she was going to do.

Jan approached and noticed that there were no cars present at the clubhouse. Well, that would make things easier. She wasn't sure if she wanted to be seen by anyone. She threw a bottle of water and a towel into her gigantic purse and made her way towards the sunning lawn.

The lawn was deserted, with chairs scattered about in haphazard fashion. A slight breeze blew the leaves of the few towering trees that provided shade from the glaring sun. Jan chose a chair situated near the clubhouse and set her towel down.

She stood there for what seemed to her an eternity, arms folded, gazing out at the view through comically oversized sunglasses, that not only provided protection for her eyes, but also some degree of anonymity. It was now or never.

After removing her sunglasses, she pulled her sweatshirt over her head, replaced her sunglasses, and stood there for a few seconds, topless but for a bra that had seen better days. She gazed down at her belly, not obese, but just a bit soft and jiggly. The sun felt good on her shoulders. She unhooked her bra and slid it off, tossing it onto the lawn chair. Her nipples stiffened at the sensation. In nearly sixty years, her breasts had never seen the sun.

She decided to take a few steps, relishing her new freedom, getting accustomed to the sensation. Though she was only half-naked, she thought it would take her a minute to take the next step. Toplessness was one thing; bottomlessness was a whole other level of exposure. Still, there was nobody else around. Though the thought of being seen naked by somebody other than her physician and her husband was titillating, she wasn't sure if she was ready. She stood for a while.

Eventually, Jan decided to go for it. She unzipped her jeans and then hooked her thumbs inside her panties, pulling both underwear and jeans down at the same time to her ankles. She kicked them off and stood totally naked, her bare feet wiggling in the cool grass. Well, that was just too much excitement. She quickly sat on her lawn chair and brought her knees up as though to protect herself. She unscrewed the lid to her water bottle and took a gulp.

After a few minutes, the initial surge of excitement wore off a bit and Jan unfolded herself to lie completely supine and vulnerable on the lawn chair. She closed her eyes and felt the warm sun bathe every inch of her skin.

She opened her eyes to a shuffling sound. The source of the sound was a man to her left trudging along, dragging his own fold-up lawn chair. Immediately, Jan felt a surge of embarrassment as the man gazed her way. What would Dale think, this preacher's wife exposing her goods to the public? Worst of all, what would the ladies of the church think? Was she sinning against God? Also, did the man like what he saw?

The man said, "Beautiful morning!" and set up his chair.

"It is," said Jan.

A bit self-consciously, Jan flipped over on her tummy. The sun began to warm her derriere. It felt glorious. She thought of her pious husband, wearing his black shirt and starched dog collar, driving his Cadillac between the homes of his parishioners, doing the work of the Lord, while she baked her naked ass in the sun. She began to drift off.

She was awoken by the need to urinate. Once she had turned onto her back, she noticed that several other folks had turned up, most basking on their lawn chairs and a few playing table tennis. Jan briefly considered slipping on her sandals and walking naked to the restroom, but then reconsidered. She had accomplished "Stationary Naked" but wasn't quite ready for "Mobile Naked" with all her bits jiggling. She dressed fully, bra, panties and all, and headed to the restroom.

After using the restroom, she paused, admired herself in the mirror, adjusted her hair, re-donned her comically large sunglasses, and headed out the door. She had errands to run in town, and she hadn't planned for a long visit anyway.

She made her way back to her chair, gathered her things, and headed to her car. All in all, she'd had a pretty good first experience being naked in public. She was sure she'd be back. She might even talk to somebody next time.

As Jan's car chugged slowly down the gravel road leading out of the park, clouds of dust billowing about, entering her open window and depositing a thin layer of debris on her dashboard and steering wheel, she spotted a naked man walking along the side of the road. He wore nothing but a straw hat that appeared quite similar to one her husband owned and a pair of gray sneakers with black socks. Then Jan noticed that the man, who was facing away from her, had a distinct mole on his left buttock.

What a coincidence that a man at the nudie park wore the same hat and had a mole in the same spot as her husband?

Before she could be seen, Jan slammed the car into reverse and zoomed in the opposite direction, finding a side road that led out of the park. At a turn-out near the entrance she spotted it—Dale's old Cadillac.

Registered at the office under the name of his deceased brother William, the Reverend Dale Parkhurst had chosen to eschew his priestly duties and spend his day enjoying the sun.

Running Bare

Finally, Wednesday afternoon rolled around, the day I was to meet with Lisa for a run. I kept anxiously looking at my phone to check the time. As 4 p.m. approached, I had anticipatory butterflies in my stomach. As I gazed out the front window of the trailer, I noticed it was overcast, a common occurrence in western Washington, even in mid-summer. As somebody once said, if you don't like the weather in Washington, just wait five minutes. It'll change.

What exactly does one wear to go on a run at a nudist camp? I hadn't thought of that. The swimming part wasn't that big of a deal. I would be nude. After all, I had just spent the afternoon a few days prior in and out of the pool wearing nothing but what the good Lord gave me. But the running part…I wasn't sure I felt too comfortable with that as I imagined my naughty bits flopping about as I ran. Somehow nude swimming seemed much more socially acceptable. Nude swimming = skinny dipping. Nude running was just…nude running. Free Running? Had I just invented a new term?

Just to be on the safe side, I decided to wear the pair of gym shorts I had on the last time I saw Lisa, a T-shirt, and a pair of running shoes I had never actually used for their intended purpose. My theory on running was that it was something one might be forced to do only when one is being chased by a bear, a saber-toothed tiger, or a jealous husband. As I have previously mentioned, I'm not very athletically inclined.

When I exited the trailer, I noted that not only was it overcast, it was also decidedly cool. I wondered if it even made sense to swim in weather like this. Talk about shrinkage.

I met Lisa at the gate to the swimming pool. She smiled and raised her coffee mug in greeting. "Hey, Brian!"

Lisa looked ready to run, with her hair pulled back in a pony-tail, earbuds hanging loosely around her neck and connected to an MP3 player strapped to her upper arm. She wore bright pink, perfectly clean running shoes but other than that was completely unencumbered by clothing.

"You ready?" she asked.

"Ready as I'll ever be."

"I think we might forgo the swim today," Lisa said, with an exaggerated frown on her face. "Not sunny like the weatherman predicted."

"We can still run, though," I said. "Or rather, I can watch you take off like a shot as I struggle to breathe yards behind you."

Lisa laughed, and it didn't seem a laugh to be polite but a full-bodied, head thrown back kind of laugh as though I was the funniest guy in the world. Without another word, she plugged her earbuds in and took off on a slow jog along the trail. I did my best to keep up.

With every step Lisa took, I could see her muscles ripple without the clothing that would usually obscure the view. Her calves were taut, her hamstrings defined. Her derriere was muscled but just slightly, pleasantly curvy. I felt like a horse following a carrot on a stick as I struggled to keep up the pace, my chest heaving and my calves burning.

As Lisa's lovely figure became smaller and smaller in the distance, I realized that, lovely though she was, her role as carrot on a stick could not overcome my pathetic aerobic conditioning. She looked back at me, red-faced and puffing as I was, and slowed down to a more reasonable jogging pace.

Lisa popped out her ear buds and grinned at me. "Tell you what, we'll make it a brisk walk." She hadn't even broken a sweat.

"I can handle that," I said, struggling to get out the words.

Lisa and I walked the outer loop. My T-shirt was drenched in sweat while she only had only the slightest hint of perspiration on her brow and upper lip. At least I could now catch my breath to be able to speak.

"Look at me, I'm drenched!" I said.

"That's one big advantage of exercising naked," said Lisa. "As soon as you sweat, it dries almost instantly—just enough to cool you off, but not enough to make you feel all nasty and damp."

"I thought it was just that I was out of shape."

"Well, there's that," said Lisa, and good-naturedly punched me in the shoulder.

Though it was overcast, the cloud cover acted as a blanket to keep in the heat of the day. It was getting pretty warm, and I took off my T-shirt with great difficulty. The sweat had made it stick to me.

"There you go," said Lisa. "You're halfway there!"

Around the next curve lay the large placid expanse of Lake Haussmann, dotted here and there with lily pads. I didn't see anybody around. A few ducks meandered about, looking for a late afternoon snack, quacking to each other.

"Feel like a swim? I changed my mind," said Lisa.

"Maybe just a quick dip would be alright."

Lisa abandoned her shoes, socks, MP3 player, and earbuds in a heap and joyfully padded barefoot across the cool grass. Now fully nude, she plunged into the cold water. I shucked my shorts, socks, and shoes, and walked to the shoreline with trepidation. I don't like being cold, but I wasn't going to chicken out in front of this lovely creature.

Incrementally, I made my way out into the lake, first up to my knees, then mid-thigh, then up to my waist. The bottom of the lake felt both silty and muddy, a pleasant cushion underneath my bare feet. I looked down at myself through the clear, clean water. My penis and testicles waved about with every slight movement in the water, free of fabric. I took a step and felt the water course around my unclad perineum and buttocks. Finally I plunged all the way in, ducking my head underwater and performing a clumsy breast stroke. For a few seconds, I was fully suspended in the water, water so cool it made me gasp as I broke through the surface again. I was enveloped in it, one with it, as every centimeter of my skin was exposed to Lake Haussmann. In the sensuous exhilaration of the moment, I felt sure I could never go back to wearing a "swimming costume." A swimming pool was pleasant, but this lake was a spiritual experience, chilly though it was.

I watched Lisa perform a variety of quite elegant moves in the water, including a backstroke, breaststroke, and on point she dove to the bottom of the lake, disappearing for a few seconds and then reappearing yards away. I was content to splash about in my own uncoordinated way.

After ten minutes or so of underwater aerobics, Lisa decided to get out. The sun was just beginning to peek out from the clouds and had cast a warm ray of light on a bench and a patch of grass. She wrung the water from her long blond hair and then sat on the bench, head thrown back, chest thrust out to greet the warm sun. Neither of us had thought to bring a towel but Lisa was content to air dry. As I exited Lake Haussmann myself and walked towards the bench, I marveled at her apparent comfort in her own skin. There she was, just as God had made her, without shame, her erect nipples softening in the sun, her long shapely legs just slightly parted to expose her unshaven vulva. There was nothing unseemly or vulgar about her posture. She was just being who she was, in the most natural and elemental form, a human being free of shame, free of pretense.

Her pubic hair, abundant and flecked with lake water, seemed to lend an even more natural and sensual quality to her. In an age when most women chose to shave some or all of their body hair, Lisa's natural appearance seemed to call even less attention to herself than it would be if all her parts were on display as a result of shaving. I recalled the women I had dated before my wife and the various ways they had styled their nether regions. There was the landing strip, the inverted triangle, the "Charlie Chaplin," as I liked to call it, and of course, the totally bare look. I did notice, however, that her legs and underarms were free of hair.

I became a bit aroused at the lovely sight in front of me and I made haste for the bench, forgoing the traditional nudist towel underneath my bottom. I didn't have one anyway. I wasn't sure if Lisa had noticed my incipient tumescence, though she did slowly and subtly bring her legs back together and sat up straighter. If she had noticed anything, she was at least kind enough not to mention it. I was still a long ways from considering myself a true nudist, I thought, able to control at will my physical reactions to lustful thoughts.

My semi-erection faded quickly and the slight breeze began to dry my skin. Within a few minutes I was completely dry. It sure beat sitting in a soggy suit, shivering, unable to change into dry clothes for fear of exposing myself in public.

I recalled the handful of times I had gone to the beach as a kid, splashing joyfully in the water, then getting cold and retreating for the sandy beach. As goosebumps formed on my arms and legs, the sand found its way into every crack and crevice of my nether regions and itched like hell. Sitting on a sopping towel in the car on the way home was a real treat as well. I never even thought to question the purpose of wearing a costume to swim.

"Well," Lisa said, "what did you think of our run?"

"I think that I very nearly died."

"Bet you would have had a better time if you'd run naked."

"I'd have a better time if I wasn't thirty pounds overweight."

Lisa cast a quick up-and-down glance at my naked body, slouched on the bench in a not-so-flattering position. "Thirty pounds? What are you talking about? You look good."

"Ah, thanks."

"Maybe ten. Maybe you could lose ten pounds."

"Well so much for your previous compliment."

"Kidding, Brian. I do have an advantage, though," said Lisa. "I've been running these trails since I was a kid. Also, every July, I go down to Tiger Mountain Nudist Park in Issaquah and do the Bare Buns Fun Run."

"Really? What is the Bare Buns Fun Run?"

"About a hundred or so of my fellow nudists run a 5K in the buff straight up Tiger Mountain. It's pretty tough, but I always

97

do well in my age category. Runners range in age from teenagers to nearly eighty. I used to see a guy we all knew as "Running Bob" scale that mountain year after year, slowly but surely. He may have been eighty, but he still did it. They even have a little mini-race for the kids. The night before they have a dance and a carbo-load spaghetti feed. It's great fun. In fact, they do one in Spokane at Kaniksu Resort and one in Vancouver B.C. at Wreck Beach."

"Sounds fun! If only I could run."

"Lots of people walk it. Nobody is too competitive, except for a group of ultra-runners, one of whom wins by a mile every year. Well, not literally a mile, but I did see one guy finish the race and start back up the mountain again!"

"Show off."

"Yeah, I might be in decent shape," said Lisa, "but nothing like those maniacs."

Lisa glanced at her wristwatch, sitting beside her on the bench, and then reached forward to don her shoes and socks. She wrapped the watch around her wrist, gathered her hair back into a ponytail and secured it with a hair tie.

"Thanks for the run," she said. "Speaking of that, I've got to run. I've got to get to work."

"Oh. Where do you work?"

"Um, long story. I'll tell you later. High five!" She slapped my hand. "I'll see you around."

I waved goodbye and then put on my damp clothing, which felt not only unpleasant but unnatural as I walked back to the trailer. Why had I bothered to dress anyway?

On top of that, when it came to Lisa, I had many more questions than I had answers. Was she interested in me as more than a casual acquaintance? What was the high-five about? Why did I feel the need to dissect and overanalyze every social interaction? It was in my blood, I guess. Once a scientist, always a scientist.

BACK TO WORK

The following day, Diane Schenck's teaching assistant called me from Skagit Valley College and asked if I were available to teach an afternoon laboratory session for the following two weeks each Tuesday and Thursday. I jumped at the opportunity and committed to the entire time period, hoping that if I were to be an engaging and knowledgeable enough instructor, I would be asked back for more work. Ultimately, I wanted to be back lecturing, where I felt at home.

The lab with which I was to assist was Anatomy and Physiology 358, covering, among other topics, the nervous and endocrine system as well as specialized organs, including the eye. The students relied heavily on computer simulations, representations of three-dimensional organs on a two-dimensional computer screen. While technology had continued to improve exponentially since my days in lab, it still fell short of the real thing—visceral, slimy, smelly actual organs. I could recall dissecting embalmed cats in my anatomy labs at the university. We hadn't the refrigeration available, so we simply sprayed down the cats with topical disinfectant and put them back on shelves in the hopes that they wouldn't rot. One group had not properly sprayed down their cat, named Ferdinand, and had been treated to a dreadful odor wafting from the anatomy lab when they arrived back from winter break. Ferdinand had turned green and purple and was thus unusable for the quarter.

When I arrived at the college, I was able to locate my class primarily by smell, the familiar odor of formalin, a preservative commonly used in anatomy labs. At high concentrations, it tended to make me cough and my eyes water, but it was also a familiar odor, letting me know I was back in my element.

The source of the formalin odor was a five-gallon bucket containing bovine oculi—cow eyes—a fair representation of human eyes, but much bigger, obviously, and easier to obtain. Each small group was given an eye to dissect, a task which most of them relished. I wandered around from group to group and pointed out such structures as the elegant choroid plexus, the gelatinous vitreous humor, and a feature absent from humans but present in cows, the tapetum lucidum, a silver layer behind the retina that allows cows and some other animals to see at night.

The students seemed interested and engaged, with the exception of a couple of kids that seemed disgusted by the idea of cutting into an eyeball, bovine or otherwise. Only one excused himself to go breathe deeply in the hallway or vomit. In my experience, those were the Physical Ed. Majors. The Pre-med or Pre-vet students were enthralled, though the eyeball experience would pale in comparison to cadaver lab, in which some of them would encounter their first real, dead human being and be forced to deal with some of the emotions associated with that. Hands and faces were always covered in a cadaver lab, because of the emotional connection associated with those body parts. It could become too real, too close to home for the students if they were to think of their anatomical specimens as former human beings who smiled, laughed, cried, and comforted.

When the lab was over after an hour, it was up to me to clean up, a task for which I was accustomed to have teaching assistants or graduate students at the university perform. The experience was both humbling and necessary, I thought, as I rinsed trays in the sink. In order to build myself back up again, I had to start from the bottom, performing menial tasks, essentially paying my penance for betraying my own sense of integrity.

The odd thing about formalin and other very strong odors is that your sense of smell gets accustomed to it fairly quickly to the point at which you no longer notice it. It seeps into your hair and clothing nonetheless, and is quite noticeable to those around you when you leave the lab. My soon-to-be-ex-wife hated that, and had always instructed me to take a shower immediately upon returning home from lab. It wasn't an unreasonable request, I'll give her that.

With the lab cleaned up and, I hoped, a satisfactory review from the students in the class, I drove home. I had about a forty-minute trip back to Deep Valley and the traffic sucked, bottle-necking up through Sedro-Woolley. My thoughts turned to Lisa. My attraction to her was undeniable, but I couldn't begin to decipher her intentions towards me. At times it seemed that she was interested but some things made me think otherwise, like the high five she had given me the other day after the run. Was she simply looking for some age-appropriate company in a community dominated by elders? Certainly, with her looks and personality, she could have anyone she wanted, and I wasn't sure if a chubby, disgraced professor was even in her wheelhouse. Still, I enjoyed the company and tried not to take our incipient friendship too seriously. My focus, I kept telling myself, should be on getting my career back on track and my drinking under control.

RUMINATION

Since her adventure at Deep Valley Nudist Park and her unexpected encounter with her husband, Jan Parkhurst had felt distinctly uneasy. Should she confront her husband with the fact that she had seen him in the altogether at a park he professed to abhor, a den of iniquity? It made no sense because it would belie the fact that she herself was there. Should she simply keep quiet and hide her secret? She wasn't sure she could keep her mouth shut in the face of Dale's hypocrisy. Jan turned from her side to her back in bed, stared at the ceiling, and wondered where in the hell her life was going.

Sequestered in his dark office, Dale Parkhurst stared at the glowing computer screen, pausing every once in a while to take a sip of his coffee, now gone cold. He looked at images of Deep Valley on a real estate multiple listing service website. An internal battle raged within him, between his moral convictions as a Christian pastor and his carnal side as a repressed sexual being who longed to break his sacred vows and experience true freedom before it was too late for him. His latest trip to Deep Valley only reinforced his confusion. He had managed to sneak in, circumventing the channels that led to his lifetime ban from the park, and for the first time in a long time, he had felt free.

Dale had the financial resources available to purchase Deep Valley. His brother had left him a considerable fortune. He could buy the land with no real difficulty and convert it to a Christian youth camp, making him the envy of pastors throughout Western Washington. He would have successfully converted a pit of sinfulness into a place of worship and wholesomeness. He could gaze down from his living room picture window onto his brainchild, Camp Parkhurst, every day, knowing that he had earned his place in Heaven. He dialed the phone number of a realtor he had known for years and set the process in motion.

CLUB MEETING

Saturday afternoon was the board meeting in which I was presumably to be sworn in as Deep Valley Nudist Club's interim president, a concept I considered rather comical. At what point, I thought, did one cross the threshold from "textile" as Security Bob put it, to full-fledged nudist? Did discarding one's clothes upon arriving home qualify one as a nudist, or did one need to socialize with other naked people? Were there different varieties of nudists? There I was, intellectualizing again.

The afternoon was brilliant and nearly eighty degrees, and after a preparatory shot of whiskey, I felt ready to take the helm of the club. Off came the shorts and T-shirt I had worn at the trailer. Naked, I slipped into a pair of flip-flops, grabbed a towel, and trudged my way to the clubhouse. If I was going to be the president of a nudist club, I would try my best to look the part.

Walking naked was an unexpected pleasure. Such a simple activity, and I had spent over thirty years with my genitals confined by cotton and denim. My penis swung freely, even joyfully, marking each step as though it were a metronome. My one regret was wearing those flimsy flip-flops, so impractical for the rutted and dusty road to the clubhouse. I now had an appreciation for the old men who trudged along Deep Valley's gravel roads, sporting nothing but white tennis shoes with black socks, such a terrible fashion statement, but undeniably practical. Had I become a nudist yet?

I walked into the clubhouse to find the other members of the council, all nude, seated at a table in the front behind nameplates. I noticed that, per nudist custom, last names were omitted from them. "Gunter K., Secretary" sat next to "Judy G., Vice President," and "Dolores E., Treasurer." There was an empty seat next to Judy. "Clara B., President" read the nameplate. I couldn't help but feel some sadness at seeing that empty seat. I hoped that it wouldn't be unoccupied that long and that Grandma would return, triumphant, to her seat on the council.

Dolores smiled at me from her seat while Gunter arose to shake my hand and then indicated for me to sit at the empty seat, the one formerly occupied by my formidable grandmother. I hesitated for a few seconds. How could I take her seat? It seemed sacrilegious. Somewhat reluctantly, I spread my towel down on the cold metal folding chair and sat. Looking out at the members located sporadically among the tables I noticed Mr. Dan, the wizened, ultra-tan proprietor of the Bare Spirits bar, Dave, the bearded hippie, and, to my delight, Lisa, who was sitting in the back, an incognito nudist, wearing shorts and a T-shirt.

After the rumbling and chitchat that usually precedes a meeting, Gunter banged his gavel and called the meeting to order. Noisily, he slurped coffee from an oversized mug, donned reading glasses, and began reading the minutes. The rest of us on the council followed along on papers that had been placed in front of us prior to the meeting. Dolores read an accounting of the budget and there was some discussion about fixing the terminally ill hot tub, but it was decided that the money wasn't available to do it.

The floor was turned back over to Gunter, who reminded lot holders to keep their lawns mowed and to have derelict golf carts either repaired or moved off premises. A motion was made to approve sending flowers and a sympathy card to the widow of a former club member who had recently died. In many ways, the meeting was indistinguishable from that of any other social club or organization.

After the usual old and new business was dealt with, I was officially voted in as the club's official interim president. All of the other members of the council pledged their support and assistance, as I had absolutely no idea what I was doing.

After the meeting, I shook hands with the other council members. Gunter informed me that I was to meet him and the others the following Saturday for executive session to discuss some private matters related to club business. It had gotten rather muggy in the clubhouse, which was not air conditioned, so it was refreshing to step outside into the sunshine. Members who had come from the meeting were busy setting up their lawn chairs, getting their towels positioned just right, their coolers by their sides, and their sunscreen applied, a task that often required the helping hand of a friend, I noticed. When one has to slather cream over the entirety of one's epidermis, it took some doing, especially for the oldest and most inflexible.

The more athletically inclined members, even if marginally so, participated in games of ladder golf, horseshoes, and pétanque, which I was beginning to realize, was a game deeply ingrained in nudist culture. Other members strode off, towels in hand, to swim or lounge by the pool for the afternoon.

I noticed Lisa standing alone, leaning against a post near the entrance to the clubhouse, sunglasses on her head, apparently scrolling through her phone like so many of the under-thirty crowd. I had a smart phone myself, but today I had no pocket to put it in. Lisa saw me in her peripheral vision, looked up, and smiled.

"Hey, Brian. Or should I say President Brian?"

I laughed. "Thanks, Lisa. It's a great, if bewildering honor."

"Did you recover okay from our run the other day?"

"Kind of sore the next day, but it wasn't too bad. I really do need to get back in shape."

Lisa looked down at her phone and appeared to be texting. I noticed what looked to be a large beeper clipped to her shorts.

"What is this, the 1990s? Is that a beeper?" I asked.

"That's my fire pager," said Lisa. She looked up again. "So, I need to run down to the fire station for some mandatory training, but I thought about doing a hike tomorrow. You want to join me?"

"Absolutely. What time to do you want to meet?"

"The earlier the better. It can get pretty hot later in the day. You want to say around eight?"

The Hike

I met Lisa at her trailer at eight o'clock the next morning, before the sun made its appearance. A chill was in the air. I stood below her front steps after knocking on her door, shivering slightly, feeling rather silly in my stunning ensemble of ankle socks, tennis shoes, and a flask tethered to my waist that was full of plain old, ordinary water. A step in the right direction was not to start the day off with a gin and tonic. As I waited for her to answer the door, I stared self-consciously at my rounded belly and parts farther south. The chilly weather was not doing my family jewels any favors. My leg hairs stood at attention. A robin chirped happily away, greeting the morning.

The front door swung open to reveal a smiling and fully clothed Lisa, hair tied back in a ponytail, a steaming cup of coffee clutched in her right hand. "Oh!" she exclaimed. "Good morning. Be right there."

"Oh," I said. "Was this not a naked hike? Why are we never reading from the same sheet of music?"

Lisa laughed. "No, no. I'll be right back."

She turned and disappeared back into the darkness of her trailer, reappearing seconds later fully nude with the exception of hiking boots and a small backpack slung over one shoulder.

"Brought us some coffee to share," she said, indicating a thermos that she held in her left hand.

"How very thoughtful of you."

"Shall I lead the way?"

"Lead away."

Lisa stowed the thermos in her pack, shut the front door behind her, and began striding ahead. "Keep up," she said. "I don't waste any time."

I did my best to keep up, huffing and puffing to the crunching of my shoes and Lisa's boots on the gravel roads that took us up a short incline and behind a water tower where the established path gave way to zigzagging narrow deer trails through the densely forested foothills.

Dew-flecked vegetation brushed my thighs and buttocks—definitely a sensation I had never experienced before as a lifelong textile. I spotted stinging nettles along the path and carefully avoided brushing against them, as I was only protected to ankle level by my socks and shoes. As a neophyte nude hiker, I certainly needed to be more cognizant of my physical environment, but the inherent vulnerability seemed to enhance my connection with nature. I wasn't just walking through it; I was part of it. Lisa remained several yards ahead of me, trucking steadily along, her well-muscled buttocks rippling as the grade of the trail increased. I hoped we would get to a point in the trail where we could walk side by side.

After about a quarter of a mile, the trail opened up a bit and we crossed a small creek by way of a log bridge. I teetered precariously on the slippery log with visions of falling and making an ass of myself but managed to cross with little difficulty. The trail widened out at that point into a logging road that continued upwards at a gradual incline and I was finally able to keep up with Lisa. She paused for a minute, took a generous slug of coffee and water and then handed me the thermos. I took a few sips of dark roasted coffee, just the way I like it, before we continued on.

The first rays of sunshine made their appearance, dappling the trail with sunlight filtered through trees, warming our butts and generally making the hike much more pleasant. I started to sweat a bit, just enough to cool me, but, as I was nude, it evaporated within seconds.

"Have you ever run into anyone on this trail?" I asked.

"Only rabbits and deer, and they don't seem to mind."

"So is this Deep Valley property?"

"No," said Lisa. "But it is forestry land and I don't think anybody else comes up here."

I hoped not to meet anybody as neither of us had brought a cover-up. If we were to run into somebody up here, it would be pretty awkward. There we would be in all our glory. I wondered what questions we might be asked. "Where are your clothes?" "Are you doing this on a dare?"

"Even so, it's good the two of us are hiking together," added Lisa. "People would probably react better to a man and a woman hiking naked together than just a single male. It's a double standard I know. A single man is considered a pervert; a man and a woman together are just enjoying a hike free of clothing."

"Have you been on many hikes like this?"

"A few. Sometimes by myself in the North Cascades and sometimes with a group of people. With a group, you've got more protection but I'm not afraid to set out by myself."

The trail became steeper and I took a few pulls off my water bottle. After a half mile or so, Lisa slowed as we approached a lookout. Several large boulders bordered a sheer drop-off. I followed Lisa as she climbed onto one of them. From our vantage point, we could look down on all of Deep Valley and the surrounding area. We could even catch a glimpse of Interstate 5 and all the cars whizzing past, appearing as small as bugs.

She glanced at me and smiled. "Beautiful up here, isn't it?"

"Sure is. Incredible view."

"Well," said Lisa. "That coffee has gone right through me. Gotta pee." Without further hesitation, she simply squatted down and began to urinate behind a bush that abutted the boulder. I averted my gaze and felt my face begin to flush.

Lisa seemed to pick up on my slight discomfort. She giggled and said, "Sorry, Brian. I've never been shy peeing in front of people. At least I picked a bush!"

Her urine stream dribbled and splashed and formed a tiny amber river that flowed down from the rocks and into the surrounding dirt, eventually soaking in. Finally, she finished and arose from her squat, doing a little dance. "Gotta shake the dew from my lily! There is really no experience quite as liberating as peeing nude in nature! You should try it, Brian."

The contrast between Lisa and my estranged wife could not have been any vaster; a woman so demure she had once farted in front of me and was so embarrassed that she had cried afterwards. And here I was spending time with a woman who seemed to have no bodily shame whatsoever.

I did need to urinate, but unlike Lisa, I have always had a shy bladder and would often stand for up to a full minute at public urinals trying to get started. I had also begun to worry that perhaps my prostate gland was enlarging. I was getting to the age where it was at least theoretically possible. I turned so my back was facing Lisa—I wasn't as bold as she - and aimed over the boulder into the valley below. After standing there awkwardly for at least thirty seconds, feeling kind of silly, stark naked, penis in hand, my stream started with a trickle and finally strengthened into a glorious off-yellow flow that arced over the boulder and off the cliff. It truly was exhilarating, liberating as Lisa had put it, possibly because it felt naughty, but also because in a really weird way, I felt even more connected with nature as I stood there releasing water back into the environment from whence it had come. Naked with the exception of shoes, there was no real border between myself and the environment.

I finished and shook off. Lisa grinned and gave me a thumbs-up. "See? Wasn't that great?" She paused a moment. "Shit. I forgot the snacks. What a bummer."

"Ah well. I need to lose weight anyway," I said. "I've burned more calories on this hike than I have for a long time."

Lisa poked me in the belly. "You don't need to lose weight, Brian."

We continued our hike for another half mile or so until we began to see signs of recent human activity—tire tracks and the presence of a much more established road that intersected our trail. We turned around at that point and headed back, stopping at the overlook to rest.

Having no towels to sit on, we plopped our bare butts on the cold, flat boulders. The sun was now directly overhead and Lisa took full advantage by lying back on the rock and basking, eyes closed, her perky nipples pointing skyward.

"So," I began. "You were going to tell me what you did for a living?"

"Oh. Yeah." She opened her eyes, shading them with her hand, and looked up at me.

"Well?"

"I'm uh…self-employed."

"Doing?"

"House cleaning."

"Why didn't you just say that in the first place?"

Lisa sighed and got up on one elbow, a position that looked severely uncomfortable on both her hips and elbows, neither of which had much padding. "Naked. I clean houses naked, Brian. I'm a nude maid." She seemed irritated that I had managed to pull this little tidbit of information out of her.

"Sorry. I didn't mean to pry."

She seemed to relax a bit. "It's okay. It's just that I've never felt totally comfortable with it. Guys gawking at me and getting paid for it. It's just one step up from being a stripper."

"Can't be that much of a leap. You're already a nudist."

"I know, but I've always been a bit of a traditional nudist. You know, the whole 'it's not about sex, it's about being comfortable in your own body' thing, so this seems a bit, I don't know, tawdry? I'm a bit of an exhibitionist at heart, but, my God, some of these outfits they want me to wear are just unreal. Skimpy French maid outfit with no panties, fishnet stockings, stiletto heels. One guy wanted me to wear just the head of a bunny costume, so that was kind of weird. I'd prefer to just be totally naked, but I accommodate each customer's particular, um…what's the word?"

"Fetish?"

"Yeah, that'll do. It's not something I plan to do forever but for now it is great money for not a lot of work.

"How much do you charge, if you don't mind me asking?"

115

"Depends. I charge ninety dollars an hour for light housework like dusting and wiping down furniture. One twenty for deep cleaning. I can clear five hundred without even breaking a sweat!"

"It kind of sounds like the ideal job for you."

"I know, right? The guys at the fire district don't know about it." She laughed. "Boy, wouldn't they flip? Some of them would probably become my best customers. Anyway, guys have always seemed to think I'm easy on the eyes, so I'm just using that to my advantage I guess."

"Well, you are easy on the eyes."

Lisa blushed and touched my knee briefly.

"So what are your plans for a career?" I said.

"I've been a volunteer firefighter for five years now. I'm an EMT and I think I'd like to take the next step and go to paramedic school. This house cleaning job is paying for my online prerequisites."

"Thanks for your help with Grandma, by the way."

"Of course. It's what I do! How is she, by the way?"

"Getting better, little by little. I imagine she'll soon be back to her old irascible self."

"Awesome," said Lisa. "Your grandmother's an institution in the club, you know that?"

"Or she should be in one!"

We sat in silence on that cold rock for a few minutes without the need to talk, feeling the sun bathe our naked bodies in warmth from above, listening to the birds chirp, feeling alive.

Finally, I screwed up my courage to ask the question I had wanted to ask for some time. Perhaps it was unnecessarily blunt, but I felt I needed to ask it anyway. "So…is this a date?"

Lisa sat up, hugging her knees. She knitted her brow. "A date? How do you mean?"

"I mean, well, is there a romantic direction to this?"

She made a sweeping gesture with her right hand. "Do you see anyone else here?"

"Just that little guy." I pointed at a chipmunk, who bounded rapidly away at my gesture.

Lisa laughed and then gazed down at her bare knees, looking pensive. She was silent for a moment. "I don't really date, Brian. I haven't had very good luck in relationships."

"Okay," I said. I figured I wouldn't push my luck any further. For now, it was glorious just feeling so connected to the earth and being in the company of such a lovely woman, feeling the breeze and the sun on my entire body.

Lisa seemed to sense my disappointment. It wasn't exactly a rejection, though it wasn't a confirmation either. She brightened a bit. "I'm glad we're getting to know each other." She paused for a moment. "And if I were the kind of person that would date, I wouldn't completely put it out of my mind to date somebody like you. How's that for an incomplete answer?" She laughed again.

"Cryptic at best," I said.

She grabbed my hand and squeezed it briefly. "Ready to head back?"

We arose and hastily wiped the dirt from our backsides. I figured I probably had some pretty unique patterns on my skin from lying on that boulder. Back down the trail we went. I had the urge to hold her hand but I figured I wouldn't push my luck any more. At least I hadn't been outright rejected and I was never a person to back down from a challenge.

When we reached Lisa's trailer, we parted ways. She asked if I wanted to hike or run again and I very willingly gave her my phone number.

"Okay," she said. "I'll call you soon. I'm not one of those people who can just sit around all day." She then gave me a hug, not a perfunctory nudist hug, but a hug in which all of our nakedness was touching, if only briefly. Her small breasts were warm and soft on my chest and she smelled just slightly of perspiration and lavender body wash. Being shorter than me, her pubic hair brushed my thighs. I moved my hips away from hers in an attempt to avoid the inevitable. When she finally pulled away from the embrace, I was already at half-mast. She turned and opened the door to her trailer. Like a good nudist, if she had noticed my arousal, she didn't say anything.

THE BOOK OF SHAME

Executive session sounded very formal but in reality it was just the four of us on the council sitting around Gunter's trailer drinking coffee, eating day-old donuts from Thrifty Foods, and discussing the latest goings-on at the club. Judy, who usually didn't speak much, brought up the topic of a long-time member who had taken to drinking way too much on weekends and being generally obnoxious. As soon as he arrived at the club after getting off at work at 5:40 on Fridays, he appeared to have not a single sober moment until late Sunday afternoon, when he would leave the park, presumably sloshed, and drive back to his home in Arlington. Judy mentioned that other campers had complained to her and others that this man would stagger into their camps and make himself at home telling off-color jokes and helping himself to other campers' alcohol until everyone packed up and went inside. Usually he got the hint at that point, but would just move on to another trailer. Judy's opinion was that it had gone on long enough and that he should be expelled from the club. Judy was a pleasant enough person, but seemed a bit intolerant as well as humor-impaired. A discussion ensued in which Dolores brought up that the member in question had contributed much to the club in previous years, such as hosting luncheons at his trailer and coordinating the annual pig roast, but that he had suffered a traumatic brain injury in the past that had changed his behavior for the worse, and that he should be spoken to privately before any official action was taken. Being so new to the council, I didn't have much of an opinion, but generally agreed with Dolores's sentiment. There was some discussion, and it was decided to give the man another chance before letting him go.

Gunter brought up the topic of the annual music festival and what bands had offered to play. Everyone but Dolores agreed that all three had been exemplary the previous year and should be brought back to play this year. Dolores said that she would be leaving the park that weekend to see her sister as loud music aggravated her. Deep Valley was her paradise, and Motown music reverberating through the walls of her trailer was not in keeping with that paradisiacal theme. There was some good-natured ribbing from the rest of the council and Dolores was a good sport about it.

As the discussion turned towards potential new members who had applied for membership, there was a knock on the door. With difficulty, Gunter hefted his three-hundred-pound body from his office chair and opened the door to reveal a man I had never met before.

Gunter shook his hand and welcomed him in. "Brian, this is Earl White. He owns Deep Valley Nudist Park. Earl, this is Brian, our interim president."

"Nice to meet you, sir," I said and shook his callused, leathery hand.

"Likewise," said Earl in a gravelly voice. He appeared to be in his mid-seventies, deeply weathered, and built like a fire hydrant. He wore a massive gray handlebar mustache that all but completely obscured his mouth. Unlike the rest of us, he was clothed in a plaid shirt, blue jeans, Stetson, cowboy boots, suspenders, and a belt buckle the size of a dinner plate.

Gunter offered him a cup of coffee but he chose not to partake. He took a seat quietly in the corner. Earl indicated with a sweep of his hand for us to continue our discussion, then sat back, arms folded, observing.

Gunter donned his reading glasses and read from a sheet of paper in front of him. "So we have an application from Steve and Laura Jacobsen," continued Gunter. "They've completed the required two visits, per club protocol." He removed his glasses and looked up. "Anybody have any comments or concerns?"

Dolores and Judy shook their heads. "Nice people," added Dolores. "I think they had mentioned they were members of a club in Oregon before moving up here to retire. She was a hospital CEO; I don't recall what he did. I think they'd fit in well here."

"Future club leadership?" quipped Gunter. Everyone laughed.

"Brian, we've already run a Washington State criminal background check to make sure these folks aren't registered sex offenders and we have also consulted our Book of Shame," said Gunter.

"Book of Shame?"

Gunter whirled around on his chair and snatched a binder from his kitchen counter. Indeed, written on the cover in large, thick, black letters was "Book of Shame." Gunter passed the book over to me.

"If inappropriate activity is reported to us, that person's name goes in the Book of Shame. You are asked to leave the premises immediately and are banned from returning. Also, your name is reported to the American Association of Nude Recreation, and you will be banned from any AANR club henceforth."

121

"Wow. You take misbehavior seriously."

"It is serious," said Gunter. "We're all about having fun, but nudists are a misunderstood culture, and we don't want people thinking it's got anything to do with sex, or swinging, or the like. Any appearance of impropriety gets you kicked out of here."

While it seemed heavy-handed, I understood the reasoning. Nudists seemed to have a poor public image, largely based on misunderstanding, and the purity of the culture needed to be preserved or it would fall into mayhem.

"So, all in favor of voting in Steve and Laura as new members?" asked Gunter.

Everyone muttered agreeably. Gunter apparently took this as a positive vote from all and scribbled something onto his notes.

From the corner of the room, Earl cleared his throat and leaned forward in his chair as if he wanted to say something. "I've got some news I need to share, and I'm sorry to have to bring it to your attention. As most of you old-timers know, Deep Creek has been around for forty-five years. We've had a good run, but the clubs aren't attracting members like they used to. It's happening all over. Membership is way down and my property taxes are just going up and up. Every year we squeak by on a shoestring budget and there's more we can't afford to repair or renovate. So…" He took a deep breath. "Unfortunately, I've decided to put the club on the market." Earl gazed around at the confused faces. "I've decided to sell Deep Creek."

Dolores looked about ready to cry. "So the club's gone? Where are we to go?"

"I'm afraid so," replied Earl. "There's a very slim chance that the park will continue to exist in its current form. Even if some members are allowed to stay, it likely won't be a nudist park anymore. I'm sorry, but I'm getting up in years and it's just more than I can continue to manage on my own."

"So how long do we have to make other arrangements?" asked Judy.

"The land is already listed with the real estate company. When we have a good offer, it will probably be in the neighborhood of ninety days for the property to be turned over to the new owner."

Gunter looked crestfallen. "I'll make the announcement at the next general membership meeting. Thanks for letting us know, Earl."

It appeared as though my term as Deep Valley Nudist Park's president was going to be much shorter than I had expected.

BACKLASH

Clad in nothing but gray tennis shoes and a wristwatch, Dolores Eisenberg bustled into the office of Deep Valley Nudist Park and plopped herself, sans towel, on one of four office chairs. She folded her hands, one of which clutched a wrinkled piece of paper atop her ample belly, and waited for her respiratory rate to decrease to normal after the hike from her trailer.

Gunter stood, leaning against the front desk, and peered at the new arrival. "Um, Dolores, you really aren't supposed to be naked here. Also, your towel?"

"I couldn't care less," Dolores said.

Gunter sighed. "What can I do for you, Dolores?"

"I've come to register a protest," said Dolores, waving the wrinkled sheet of paper. "I have no intent on having a pervert take over this park."

Gunter looked quizzical. "I'm sorry. What's this all about?"

"I demand to speak to Earl White," said Dolores. "I would rather die here than have some moralistic maniac take over our park."

"I'm still confused."

"That pastor, Dale Parkhurst, wants to buy Deep Valley. He's a pervert and a generally awful man. I'm sure he'll kick us all out and build God-knows-what here. Well, I won't have it." Dolores became more worked up, the color rising in her cheeks.

Gunter worried that her blood pressure would soon rise to the point of short-circuiting her brain. "What's this paper about?" he asked, indicating the sheet of paper that Dolores was now frantically using to fan herself.

"It's a petition, signed by twenty-six members, asking Earl to please not entertain any offers from Dale Parkhurst."

"Earl is out of town, but I'll see that he gets this. I'll call him as well, but I have to tell you, it might not do any good. I love this place as much as you do, Dolores, but we're getting old too, and it may not be that long before we have to think about a retirement home."

"I'd rather croak!"

"I'm sorry, Dolores. I'll do my best to reason with Earl."

Dolores nodded, braced herself with both hands on the arms of the chair and hoisted herself up. "Goddamn, Gunter. Do you think you could come up with less comfortable chairs?"

Gunter chuckled. Dolores turned around to walk out the door, the imprint of the fabric creating an interesting design on her bare backside.

With dismay, Gunter noticed that the chair Dolores had sat in, sans towel, was now the recipient of a rather large sweat stain.

A Chat with Lisa

Lisa called me on Sunday. "Did you hear about the club?" she asked.

"That it's being sold?"

"Yeah, that's crazy. Do you think they'll sell to a nudist?"

"I doubt it. The owner is being forced to sell. I think he'll take the first good offer that comes along."

"Shit. I guess that means I'm going to have to find another place to live."

"Yeah. Me too. Couldn't have come at a worse time for either of us, but I'm more worried about my grandma. The club is her life. The last thing she'd want is to be stuck in a retirement home with a bunch of 'old farts' as she so delicately puts it."

"Ugh. And Dolores? I think she'd rather wither up and die than to ever leave this place. On the other hand, I think she has money, so it will be easier for her. I think some people live at nudist campgrounds simply because it's cheap housing."

"Yeah? Never thought of that. I guess there are some people that I've never seen naked here, come to think of it."

"Oh, you mean like Bob and those silly shorts of his?" said Lisa. "It's not like I want to see him naked. I just don't see why he doesn't join in."

"True. Well, hopefully there will be some time for all of us to get our plans in order before the place is sold."

"Yeah. I don't have a pot to piss in. I live in my parent's trailer. Guess they'll have to sell it or I'll just have to tow it to some other trailer park. The thought of living somewhere where I need to wear clothes all the time is fucking depressing." Lisa paused. "Anyway, onto happier subjects…Have you ever been to a nude beach before?"

"I thought we already had."

"Oh, yeah. Lake Haussmann. Well that's kind of a nude beach, but I'm thinking more of an ocean beach."

"We have those around here?"

"Not officially sanctioned, no. But there are a handful of them up and down the Puget Sound that have been unofficial for years and generally tolerated by the locals. Would you like to go?"

"When were you thinking of going?"

"I've got tomorrow off and the next day."

"I've got a lot of errands to run tomorrow and I need to teach lab Tuesday, but I could go later in the day I guess or do it the next day."

"Oh, that's right, you're teaching. How is that going, by the way?"

"Good. I'm really enjoying it."

"At the college, right?"

"Yep. Class ends at noon, so maybe we could go after that?"

"Sounds great. Maybe I could meet you at the college. We could grab lunch somewhere, then head up. It's up in the Bellingham area, so it's not that far."

"It's a deal," I said.

"Awesome! I've got some friends I want you to meet."

DOGFISH POINT

Tuesday I had to remind myself to slow down and focus on my students. This was difficult, as my mind kept going back to Lisa and our imminent trip to the beach. Once class let out, I walked out into the parking lot to meet Lisa standing by her vehicle. It occurred to me that I had never before seen her drive anything other than a golf cart around Deep Valley. Her truck was a lifted black Dodge Ram 3500 full size pickup and looked to be fairly new. Business must be good, I thought. Lisa was wearing tight blue jeans, hiking boots, and a rather shapeless sweatshirt. Her hair was tied back in a simple ponytail and she wore a beat-up baseball cap lettered with "Cato Excavation."

She greeted me with a warm hug, longer than the "nudist hug" that people exchanged at Deep Valley, a sort of mutual back-patting with groins apart. Her shampoo smelled floral and I noticed that she wore small gold hoop earrings.

"My rig or yours?" she asked.

"Either way."

"I'll drive then since I know the way."

I climbed into the passenger's seat. The truck looked clean on the outside but was a disaster inside. Lisa swept aside a pile of

Starbucks containers, cosmetics, and what looked at a glance like parking tickets. "There's a spot for ya. Sorry for the mess."

"No big deal. Nice truck, though," I remarked, though internally I cringed. My OCD was being triggered massively. If there was one thing I couldn't stand, it was a messy house. Next to that was a messy car. I wondered at how somebody who makes her living as a maid or housekeeper could be so disorganized in her personal life. As beautiful and pleasant as Lisa was, though, it was easy to forgive her.

"Thanks. It's my dad's. He left it for me to use when he and my mom moved down to Arizona a couple of years ago." She shoved her hat down a little bit farther to shield her eyes from the sun. "In fact, this hat is his. I guess he'd left it in the truck." She squinted. "Forgot my damn sunglasses. I'm annoyed. Check the glove compartment for me, will you?"

I popped open the glove compartment and out popped three pairs of sunglasses, along with a couple of gift cards, a wad of napkins, and an ice scraper. "Any of these work?"

"Thanks," said Lisa. "They're cheap and scratched, but they'll work. Where do you feel like getting food?"

"Mexican?"

"Nah. Gives me the shits."

"Buffet?"

"Meh. Not that hungry."

"Thai food?"

"Now you're talking."

I gave Lisa directions to a little hole in the wall Thai place I know in downtown Mount Vernon. It was about the size of a closet, but had amazing food. It was, however, claustrophobic, as its popularity had exceeded its square footage. As Lisa drove and tried to listen to my convoluted directions, she turned down her radio that had been blaring some particularly awful Top 40 music. I caught myself glancing over at her a bit too often and hoped she wouldn't notice. She looked almost as good in clothes as she did out of them. This was the first time we had actually met each other outside of Deep Valley.

Lisa somehow managed to skillfully parallel park her monstrosity of a truck in an area where street parking was at a minimum. I was impressed, as my method of finding a parking spot when in town was to circle the block until I saw reverse lights on a vehicle occupying a head-in spot. Her vehicle was a hell of a lot bigger than mine.

Once we got inside the restaurant, I warned Lisa about how spicy the food could be. "Don't order anything more than a one star. Way too spicy. You'll experience it twice, once going in and once coming out."

Lisa nodded, then ignored me and ordered three stars, smiling slyly as she did so.

"You're braver than I am," I said.

She ordered Pad Kee Mao and I went with my standby, Pad Thai with one star. I was nothing if not a creature of routine.

Conversation was next to impossible between the seating arrangement and the noise. Lisa wolfed down her food with gusto, appearing unaffected by how spicy the food was that she had ordered. We attempted some rambling dialogue in which we discussed Thai food and Asian food in general. I went off on some tangent about Kim Chee and how my ex-girlfriend was Korean and probably still is. Lisa laughed until her eyes watered and she nearly choked. She sipped on her water while I finished my Pad Thai at a slightly slower pace.

When we had finished our meal, we climbed back into her truck and started heading northbound on Interstate 5, getting off at the Chuckanut Drive exit, stopping briefly to grab beer and snacks and then heading up the highway itself. State Route 11/Chuckanut drive is a long, winding, narrow road bordered to the east by steep hillside and to the west by Chuckanut Bay. It was a beautiful, if a bit precarious drive, with large vehicles passing in the opposite direction with just inches between us and them.

Lisa pulled over at an unmarked turnout and shut off the engine. "Ready for a hike?"

I hadn't anticipated a hike. All I was told was that we were visiting a nude beach. "Not exactly," I said.

"Don't worry. Downhill isn't bad. Just watch your footing. It's coming back up again that's a bit of a bitch. They can't make it too easy to get to or every yahoo in this county would come down here and invade our peace and quiet."

We grabbed our beer, snacks, a couple of towels, and sunscreen and shoved everything into a backpack that Lisa had brought with her. I offered to shoulder the load down to the beach. It was the least I could do, as I didn't feel like being completely emasculated. Lisa led the way down a narrow path that became much steeper very quickly.

"Sometimes I get naked right here," said Lisa, as we passed a small lookout. "I almost never run into anybody on this trail and if I do, it's somebody on the way down to the nude beach or up from it so it's not a big deal. Lisa opted not to disrobe though, and we continued down the steep trail, through the cool forest, under a tree branch, through spider webs, and down a makeshift staircase until we arrived at the railroad tracks.

131

"Almost there," said Lisa.

"I was hoping so," I said, beginning to breathe hard.

We walked the tracks northbound and I noticed a sign stating "BNSF Property. Keep Off."

"Yeah, this isn't totally legal," said Lisa, noticing my concern. "If you see a pickup coming down the track, you need to get off quickly. The railroad gives tickets for trespassing. I haven't gotten one yet, but I've known people who have. Obviously, you have to pay attention to the trains. You'll hear a whistling sound in the tracks and then you have about eight seconds to get off or you'll be a locomotive's hood ornament."

"Well, that's reassuring."

Lisa laughed. "Don't worry. You'll be fine. You've just got to keep your eyes and ears open. I've seen people walk the tracks with headphones on and I'm like, really, are you that stupid?"

We turned the corner and there it was, the nude beach, as evidenced by the lone nude man standing atop a large rock, arms folded, staring off at the water. Lisa and I descended a stone staircase to a gravel area flanked by flat slate stones in the shape of a large U-shaped bench.

"Is this okay?" asked Lisa. "This is where I usually sit."

"Sure." I doffed the backpack and set it down on the stone bench.

Lisa unzipped the backpack, removed a pink towel, and laid it down on the stones, preparing her spot. Then she stripped. She was naked within twenty seconds. "Ah," she said. "So much better." She fished around in the pack for a beer and cracked it open. "It's after noon, right? Beer o'clock," she said. I took my clothes off as well and laid them out beside her towel.

"Want to walk around? I'll give you a tour of the place." Lisa slipped on a pair of water socks with heavy soles. "You really need to protect your feet here. Barnacles everywhere." I grabbed a beer from the backpack, cracked it open, and followed Lisa. I kept my tennis shoes on. The beach was beautiful, but a far cry from a tropical sandy beach. Barnacle-encrusted rocks, ground sea shells, and kelp beds dominated the place.

"This area is known as the Hot Box," said Lisa, indicating the stone bench where she had laid our belongings. "It can get really warm here mid-afternoon when the sun warms up the rocks and it's also sheltered from the wind. It's where the old-timers hang out, the regulars, those who have earned the respect of others over time. I'm an honorary old-timer. Everything you see here has been built by the first old-timers over years, rock by rock. Some of the old-timers are still around." The tide was fairly low and Lisa pointed out a man out on the tide flats using a crowbar to very slowly leverage a huge boulder from where it had been to the manmade bulkhead that protected the sunning areas from winter storms. "And they're still building it," added Lisa. "There are always repairs to be made, especially at the beginning of the season when they repair what the winter storms have damaged. It's like a career for some of these guys."

Towards the water were a couple of other raised sunning areas, bolstered by large boulders to protect them from the winter tides. Gentle waves lapped against the pebbled shore.

Lisa pointed at where the man still stood, contemplating the water. "This is Dogfish Point and I think that's Kevin standing there. Bit of an odd duck. Picks up dead bodies for a living. Nice guy, though. Sometimes he kayaks in here. He's got one of those pedal kayaks. It's really cool. As far as I know, he kayaks naked all the way from the Larrabee boat launch."

We took a narrow trail through some brush and came out onto another beach area, this one more expansive, though lacking the extensive rock work of the other side. Large pieces of driftwood served as seat backs or benches for a couple of other sunning areas. We walked past the driftwood to another rocky outcropping and a narrow rock formation that extended out into the sea. Lisa pointed at an indentation in the rocks flanked by a low rock wall. "That's known as Judy's Cave," she said. "I have no idea who Judy is or was. Maybe she doesn't come down here anymore, but people sometimes stake out an area and make it their own. Around the corner is Wayne's World. Wayne still comes down from time to time."

There was, in fact, a handmade sign that read "Wayne's World" attached to a stick jammed between two large rocks. Wayne wasn't in his world, but a very pretty young lady was, face down on her towel, enjoying the sun, a half-drunk bottle of Corona beside her. Wayne's World was defined by a low rock wall constructed, presumably, of found rocks that fit together like a jigsaw puzzle.

"When the tide's out, you can walk for a couple of miles up the beach to the border of Larrabee State Park. Sometimes nudists hang out further up. Not everybody wants to be social all the time."

"Can you walk naked?"

"Yeah, but most people bring a cover-up with them. It's not officially nude, and we don't want to get into any trouble. Always cover up if you see kids."

"Good to know."

The tide was fairly far in, so we had enough room to walk along the beach, but not much farther in either direction. Broken clam, mussel, and barnacle shells crunched under our feet. The slight breeze, carrying with it the briny smell of the ocean, was refreshing on such a sunny and warm day.

"We could swim later, if you're brave," said Lisa, with a smirk. "But you've got to be careful and know the lay of the land. Bump your knee against a barnacle-covered rock underwater and you'll be a bloody mess. That's known as a rookie mistake."

"Sounds delightful. I'll be sure to take you up on your offer," I said sarcastically.

Lisa and I crunched back to the Hot Box where she had set her towel and I immediately noticed the temperature difference. I set my towel down as well, leaning against a flat rock that conformed perfectly to my back and within a few minutes had sweat dripping down my chest. We sipped our beers and listened to the waves gently lap the shore. Beer wasn't a very good way to hydrate, and I knew I would pay for my beach adventure today with a headache tonight. I should have bought some cheap bottled water along with the twelve-pack of Coors light that I was sure Lisa and I would fully consume between the two of us.

One beer turned into another, and then another. At around 2:00, I spotted a figure walking along the track towards the beach with a walking stick in his hand. Every once in a while, he would pause and appear to nudge a wayward rock or piece of garbage out of the way with the stick. As he approached, I noticed that he was a thin man with a broad-brimmed hat and large glasses. He descended the staircase and placed his walking stick down, which turned out to consist of a ragged umbrella wrapped with duct tape. He set down his backpack and sat for a minute, catching his breath.

"Hey, Bruce," said Lisa.

"Lisa, what's going on?"

"Bruce, this is Brian. Brian, Bruce. Bruce is one of the elders here at the beach. He's been here decades. He's like the mayor of the beach."

I shook the older man's hand. The firmness of his handshake belied his small size. "Nice to meet you," he said. "I'm one of a few old guys that watch over this beach."

Bruce slowly removed his clothing. He didn't appear to have an ounce of fat on him and was dark bronze from head to toe. He looked to be about seventy years of age, but a healthy seventy. I decided it wasn't possible to make the trip to the beach unless you are in semi-decent shape.

Bruce chatted with us for a while, then cracked open a beer and wandered over to the other side. Throughout the course of the afternoon, a few more people trickled in, mostly older, single men, but a few couples and a group of three college-aged girls who seemed to be a bit intoxicated when they arrived, even more so after they got naked and began imbibing red wine and splashing happily about in the shallow water. I did enjoy watching them frolic about, but I had all I needed in Lisa, sitting next to me, bronzing in the sun.

As the afternoon wore on, people filtered in, cracked open beers, smoked marijuana, and chatted with each other before going off to their own little sanctuaries of solitude among the rocks. The senior beach bums appeared almost as though they were commuting into work, saying their hellos and then setting up in their favorite spots. The beach was its own little community, made by and for naked people, hidden from view and unknown but to a few eccentric folks who called this beach their own.

"Everybody has a nickname down here," said Lisa. "There's Cell Phone Mark, who's always on his phone, Taco Rick used to bring tacos down here, Guitar Mark packs a guitar all the way down here and strums away. Even some people who've only come down here once or twice have acquired nicknames. I remember Bruce telling me about "The Sidler." He was this guy that kept moving his towel closer and closer to single girls on the beach, thinking they wouldn't notice."

"That's hilarious. How could he think they didn't notice?"

Lisa laughed. "Overly convinced of his own sneakiness, I guess. There used to be this guy that would come down and talk to me while I was lying on my towel, which would have been fine except that he stood there the whole time with his arms folded and his dick hanging right in my face. It's like, okay, dude, I know you have a dick. I just don't need to see it from that perspective."

"Seems kind of rude."

"It is a little offensive. Most of those people don't last long, though. They decide they aren't going to find what they're looking for here or they get kicked out by the old-timers."

While we were there, a younger man wandered in, disrobed, and then began staring at the three young women while casually fondling his small and semi-flaccid member. His visit did not last long. Bruce approached him and presumably said some things to him that made him supremely uncomfortable. Shortly thereafter the man put his clothes back on and left.

"The seniors don't allow inappropriate behavior on the beach," said Lisa. "If you want to come here and stroke your wood and make people uncomfortable, you get told to leave. That's what I appreciate about this place. I can feel safe as a woman down here. In fact, I've called out a couple of people who are being inappropriate. This place is just about being yourself and enjoying the sun. It's not a place to gawk or to try to look for a girlfriend, or a boyfriend for that matter. We have a pretty sizable gay population here. Usually they hang out on the far side."

We stayed until late in the afternoon, at which point I was pleasantly buzzed on four Coors Lights, during which time Lisa had ventured out into the water a couple of times, re-emerging smelling of the sea and streaked with seaweed but remarkably unscathed by barnacles, like a true veteran of a Northwest nude beach. Finally, with some liquid encouragement, I waded out there myself, though with no small amount of trepidation. Once I had achieved flotation, I was able to allow the current to take me around Dogfish Point, from one side of the beach to the other. I did float much better in salt water than in fresh. Shivering and with seaweed clinging to my legs, I arrived back on the south side of the beach. The water was so cold I hadn't even noticed I had met a barnacle or two with my shin. It stung a bit, but not for long.

Getting from the beach back to our car was a challenge in and of itself. The day of sun and the beers did not make it easier. What had been a fairly easy downhill trip became an absolute slog in the opposite direction and I wondered how people thirty years older than myself could complete the hike without dying halfway there. Now clothed and drenched in sweat, sunscreen smeared and dripping, we arrived huffing and puffing at Lisa's truck. At least Lisa had been kind enough to walk ahead of me at a slow clip, so that I could catch up without going into cardiac arrest halfway up.

Lisa drove with both front windows down in her truck on the way back to the college. Traffic had thickened and the Boulevard leading to Skagit Valley College had become a bottleneck. This gave us plenty of time to chat and allowed our sweaty T-shirts to dry. Lisa had thrown her "Cato Excavation" hat up onto the dash to allow her hair to dry freely.

"So, was your dad in the excavation business?" I asked.

"Yep. Family business actually. My dad ran the day-to-day operations with his brother and my mom did the accounting. Finally, they got sick and tired of the wet, cold winters up here so they decided to retire to Arizona and sold their half of the business to my uncle. He still runs it, based out of Stanwood down south and has done really well for himself."

"How do your parents like Arizona?"

"They love it, apparently. I've been down to see them a couple of times. They were long-time members at Deep Valley so, not surprisingly, they are in a nudist resort down there, too, Mira Vista Resort. It's nice. Hot down there, though, so they come up to Deep Valley to visit pretty often in the summer."

"I haven't spent much time in Arizona. Sounds nice, though. I'm originally from Northern California, so it took me a while to get used to the winters up here in the Northwest. Going to work in the dark, coming home in the dark, not seeing the sun for days…weeks even, the endless rain. I never could understand why everybody was so friendly and cheerful, even though they're soaked to the skin. And what's up with never using an umbrella?"

"Oh yeah, no true resident of greater Seattle uses an umbrella. We don't tan. We rust! I'm from here, but I hibernate in the winter," said Lisa. "I watch movies, read books. Just can't bring myself to hike or run naked in the rain!"

139

"You could wear clothes, I guess."

Lisa laughed. "Oh, that's no fun, Brian."

Traffic continued at a crawl, but I didn't mind as I was enjoying getting to know Lisa a bit better. The sun and slight breeze had dried our clothing and it began to be more pleasant. Lisa had turned down her radio station, mercifully, to be able to talk with me, and we just enjoyed each other's company.

Lisa was silent for a couple of minutes and then spoke up. "Brian, you never told me much about yourself. What's your background?"

Now that was a subject I knew would need to be broached eventually, but I felt rather captive in this truck inching along at a snail's pace through traffic. I could lie, but I felt that our nascent friendship might eventually morph into something more. If I lied to her now, she would eventually have to learn the truth and by then the trust would have been broken. I took a deep breath and began, electing to tell my sad story in small, bite-sized parcels.

"You know I told you I'm a lab assistant at Skagit Valley College?"

"Yeah. That's cool."

"Well, there's a bit more to the story. I'm actually a professor."

"Like a doctor?"

"I have a Ph.D., yes."

"Wow. I'm impressed, Brian! What's your Ph.D. in?"

"Cellular and molecular biology. I've also taught anatomy and physiology quite extensively. The thing is…"

"Yes? I'm all ears."

"Well, I was teaching up at Western and well…"

"Yes? Yes?" Lisa seemed mildly amused by my hesitation. I could tell from looking at her in my peripheral vision that she was smirking slightly.

Another deep breath. "I have a problem with alcohol, Lisa. I was going through a separation and was very stressed out. So I turned to alcohol. Actually, that's not entirely true. I have had an alcohol problem for years. It affected my marriage deeply. The more I drank, the worse our marriage became. Well, I came to work under the influence. The administration wasn't amused and, I got fired."

"Hmmm." Lisa's smirk had disappeared. She was silent for what seemed an eternity and I felt compelled to fill the void in our conversation somehow. But was it to alleviate my discomfort or hers?

"So," I began. I was winging it. "I'm working through my issues. I fully intend to go back to teaching full time. My research..."

Lisa kept her left hand on the wheel and put her right on my knee briefly. One of a long series of traffic lights turned green. "Brian," she said, "it's okay. I don't think any less of you. Nobody can take away your accomplishments. I mean, shit, I'm not smart enough to be a doctor."

"Sure you are."

"I dunno. Maybe it's just a lack of motivation. But anyway, don't be ashamed of what you've done in your past. Just look forward to the future."

I felt as though a huge weight had been lifted from my shoulders, but it didn't relieve me from the responsibility of changing my ways and making sure something like that never happened again.

Finally we made it through the gauntlet of Burlington Boulevard, across the bridge and onto College Way towards the college. Traffic moved a little more quickly now, despite a train passing through. We rode along in companionable silence until Lisa pulled into the parking lot at Skagit Valley College.

"I'd love to hang out," said Lisa. "But I've got drill for the fire department tonight. I'll call you tomorrow, okay?"

As I took off my seatbelt and prepared to leave Lisa's car for mine, she gave me a quick peck on the cheek. As the over-analytical, neurotic wreck that I could be at times, I wondered if she felt some pity for me as a disgraced ex-professor or if it was a sign of genuine affection.

As I drove home, my head began to throb from the combined effects of dehydration and beer. Beer didn't do to me what hard alcohol did in terms of a lack of judgment and coordination, though I was fairly sure if I had a tail-light out or failed to signal and was pulled over by the Skagit County Sheriff's Office, I would reek of beer and find myself in worse trouble than I was before.

I made it safely back to Grandma's trailer, thanking God, the Universe, or any other convenient deity for making it home intact.

Then I did what any reasonable person who'd just spent the day swilling beers on the beach would do. I made myself a gin and tonic and passed out in front of the television.

Hungover

I awoke to a headache the likes of which I had rarely before experienced. "Hangover" would be too benign of a term.It felt as though my brain had expanded to twice its size and was trying to escape from my skull. Each heartbeat created a pulsation in my head that was nearly unbearable.

As I arose from bed and weaved my way to the bathroom, it seemed as though the entire percussion section of a full orchestra was banging away on my skull from the inside. I cursed my poor decision to drink so many beers without hydrating at the same time as I tossed 800 mg of Ibuprofen into my mouth and washed them down with a swig of water. I dry-heaved for a few agonizing seconds into the sink. Then I went back to bed. Clearly today would not be very productive.

Something needed to be done about my alcohol intake, I thought to myself. I was always hesitant to commit to the title "alcoholic" but perhaps I was just playing mental gymnastics with myself in order to avoid coming to terms with the depth of my problem. I had gone days without alcohol in the past and never experienced any withdrawal symptoms. I didn't shake, I was never assaultive, and I never experienced a blackout. If I had a mental image of an alcoholic, it would be of a lonely man in a dark room swilling vodka from the bottle at ten in the morning, never someone like myself, educated and ostensibly successful, or formerly so. Still, my enthusiasm for the bottle had cost me a job, my marriage, and possibly a career.

What was I to do? AA didn't seem my style, sitting in a round, droning on about my problems, so much worse than anyone else's. Therapy had done me no good in the past. I'd tried previously to limit myself to drinking only two days a week, but would inevitably come up with some excuse to drink on any another day. Why not? It's President's Day. It's my dog's birthday. A friend I hadn't seen in a while was coming over. Just one. No more. Soon I'd slouch back into my old habits.

As I laid in bed, trying to remain perfectly still for fear of once again starting up the percussion section of the orchestra, I resolved to quit drinking alcohol—at least for now. What day was it? July 15? As good a day as any to start my experiment with sobriety. Shall I say…a month? Come on, Brian, make it two months, September 15, the unofficial end of summer in the greater Seattle area.

After about an hour of lying in bed, the Ibuprofen kicked in, and I was able to get up and brew some coffee. Now, what should I do with my alcohol-free day?

I hadn't seen Grandma in a few days and since the last time I had visited, she had been transported via Northwest Ambulance to a nursing facility known as Life Care of Skagit Valley in the small town of Sedro-Woolley. It was more convenient to get to than Skagit Valley Hospital as it was only thirty minutes or so west of Deep Valley. I decided to head down there, hangover or not.

I have never liked nursing homes and I suppose there would be something wrong with me if I did. I had watched my great-grandparents wither away to nothing in a nursing home when I was a kid and had been spooked when an old, demented lady grabbed my arm in the hallway and implored me to help her, a look of terror and utter confusion on her face. The smells, the moans, the twisted bodies slumped in wheelchairs in the hallways could be quite frightening for a young child.

So it was with some trepidation that I crossed the threshold of Life Care of Skagit Valley and entered the overheated environment of warehoused senior citizens, many waiting to die, and some retaining some hope of rehabilitation. I hoped that my grandmother would be in the latter category.

I stopped at the desk and a nursing assistant directed me to Grandma's room. As I turned a corner, I spotted her, slowly trucking down the hallway with the assistance of a walker. With one hand she was attempting to steer the thing, equipped with tennis balls on the feet and all, and in the other hand she held her old dingy plastic gas station coffee mug that she had used ever since I'd known her, a coffee cup that had never been washed, to my knowledge, and had a thick brown patina on the inside. While her one-handed approach wasn't the safest way for Grandma to ambulate, I was pleasantly surprised and pleased to see her not only up and walking but at least partially able to use all her limbs.

"Hi Grandma," I said.

"Brian." She tipped her coffee cup in greeting, spilling a good deal of it, and wavered a bit as she attempted to balance.

"Let me get that for you, Grandma." I took her coffee cup from her so she wouldn't fall over. "I'll hand it to you when you want a sip." She nodded. "Well, how are you?" I asked.

"How do you think? My roommate died the first night I was here and the food is like warm diarrhea."

"Well, I'm pleased to see you've regained your sarcastic attitude. I'm sorry to hear your roommate died."

"It's alright," said Grandma. Her speech was slurred but intelligible, though she seemed to be having a bit of difficulty articulating all her syllables. "She was 104 years old or something. I couldn't get any sleep. The aides kept coming in, flicking on lights, turning the old gal her in bed and whatnot. The funeral guys came in at about 3:00 and made a bunch of noise. Anyway, I gotta sit down."

Grandma sat in one of the many chairs lined up in the hallway for just that purpose, for residents who needed a rest on the way to their destinations. She sighed and took her coffee cup back. I noticed that the fingers of her right hand curled in an unnatural way around the handle. Her grip was tenuous.

"You seem to be doing incredibly well, Grandma. Your speech is back, you can walk. Your attitude hasn't changed. I'm really pleased."

"I still can't remember shit. Have trouble finding words sometimes. My hip is alright, I guess. Couple times a day I go to…what are those classes where they help you get better?"

"You mean physical therapy."

"That's it. Twice a day. I don't like that girl. She treats me like an old lady."

"Well…"

"Watch it, Brian. You're only as old as you feel."

"And how old do you feel, Grandma?'

146

"About a hunnert and twenty on a good day." She managed a chuckle that preceded a coughing fit. "Still can't swallow very well. Did you notice the coffee?"

She handed me the cup and I swirled it around. It seemed to have the consistency of syrup.

"They thicken it," said Grandma. "Apparently I'm on swallowing precautions on account of my stroke. Isn't that just nasty? Blech. I'm not giving up my coffee though, even if I have to chew it. I ain't smoking, though. Got one of them patches."

"Awesome, Grandma."

A nurse pushing a med cart made her way down the hallway, dodging slowly moving residents creating mini-traffic jams with their wheelchairs. An unpleasant smell wafted from a nearby room and a nursing assistant exited a short while later, her hands gloved, carrying a full plastic bag.

"I'm busting out of here as soon as I can. At least I'm not shittin' myself like most of these poor old farts. I get up on the commode. Need help wiping my ass, though. I guess that'll come back with time." Grandma took another swill of her syrupy coffee. "Anyway, how's life back at my house?"

"Well, there's a bit of news, actually. Deep Valley is being sold."

"What? You've gotta be kidding. Who are they going to sell it to?"

"Nobody knows yet. Apparently I'm the interim president until you get back on your feet. Earl White said that it's because of financial trouble he has to sell."

"Well, shit."

"That's about what Lisa said."

Grandma raised the only eyebrow she was capable of raising. "Lisa, huh? You've been talking to her, then?"

"We've spent some time together, yeah. She's trying to kill me by taking me on hikes and runs, but I'd like to get to know her better."

"You and every other male at Deep Valley".

"I'm sure you're right, as always, Grandma."

We visited a bit longer until Grandma announced that she needed to poop. It was also getting to be about lunch time. I took that as my cue to take my leave. I helped her to her feet, steadied her until she found her balance, and hugged her frail, bony frame. We rarely embraced, as Grandma had always been a bit prickly, but I felt it was appropriate, considering her fragile state. I was surprised at how insubstantial she felt in my embrace, barely held together by bones and sinews, belying her often bombastic personality.

I walked out the door to sunshine and a warm, refreshing breeze. An old man sat just outside the front doors, bundled up in layers, a cigarette dangling from his toothless lips, an oxygen cannula sitting in his lap. A transit bus sat idling in the pass through, its wheelchair ramp down, dropping off another resident. The prospect of aging filled me with dread. I wasted no time getting in my car and zooming out of there.

HOPE

Dr. Yonemitsu, my old department head from Western, rang me up on Thursday. I looked at the caller ID and considered not answering at all, since our last interaction had not been a positive one. I decided at about the fourth ring to pick up.

"Hello?"

"Hi, Brian, it's Henry."

"Hello Dr. Yonemitsu."

"Just call me Henry as you always have. You're still a colleague. I just phoned to see how you're holding up."

"Getting by, Henry. Doing some part-time work."

"Great! Where are you working now?"

"I'm teaching lab and substituting for some lectures at Skagit Valley College."

"Are you working on getting healthy?" I knew exactly what Henry meant when he said that. It was a euphemism for "have you quit drinking?"

"Every day, Henry. I have resolved to quit drinking alcohol." Even as those words escaped my lips, I didn't really believe them. Had I truly resolved to quit drinking alcohol or was I just barely able to maintain a dry spell of more than a day? If I didn't believe my own words, why would Henry?

"That's great to hear," said Dr. Yonemitsu. "It was never my desire to let you go, but my hand was forced. You know how upper administration can be. That being said, though, I have been mulling an opportunity for you, Brian, come fall quarter. The university is looking into offering online lectures and I'm wondering if you might be interested."

"Of course."

"Now, it wouldn't be near the compensation you received as a full-time professor, but it would be a start. Maybe after some time, you could work yourself back into a full-time post."

I mulled the new information about in my head, considering the pros and realizing there were very few cons to the deal. Despite my embarrassment at being unceremoniously sacked by a department head who hadn't taught any classes in over ten years, I was willing to eat crow, even if it meant clambering up from mid-career.

"Brian?"

"Yes, Henry, most definitely. I would be very interested."

"I will keep you posted. Dr. McNulty has taken over your classes, but he is looking to retire soon. I just want to make sure you get healthy and sober before you return."

I thanked Dr. Yonemitsu and concluded the call, pleased that even if I had to look for a new place to live, at least I might be able to eventually revive my floundering career.

A Visit with Lisa

My phone rang in the middle of my customary mid-afternoon nap. I picked it up and my heart did a flip-flop when I saw the caller ID: Lisa. I tried not to seem too eager and waited four rings to pick up.

"Hey, you," said Lisa. "Did I catch you at a bad time?"

"Of course not. It's never a bad time when you call."

"Well, aren't you a charmer. So, are you busy tonight?"

"Nothing planned so far."

"Do you feel like coming over to my humble abode and having a drink?"

"I'd be glad to, if you've got coffee brewing. You can have a drink for me."

"Oh. Sure. Are you not drinking?"

"I'm trying to quit drinking, believe it or not."

"Right on, Brian. I'm proud of you and I'll try not to corrupt you. That is, unless you want me to. Do you mind if I have a glass of wine?"

"Not at all."

"See you at about seven? Maybe bring a snack or something?"

At six thirty that evening, I jumped in the shower and then readied myself for what I was increasingly sure was something resembling a date with the lovely Lisa. I stood naked in front of the mirror and peered at myself from all conceivable angles, including the X-rated ones, before picking out a suitable button-up shirt and pair of slacks. I'd taken to "going commando" as of late, so I eschewed the undergarments. I thought to myself how ridiculous it seemed to be dressing up to go on a date with a nudist at a nudist campground. I suppose I was still a bit of a textile.

It was a warm evening and Lisa's front door was wide open when I arrived with just the screen door closed, saving me the trouble of knocking on the door and then pacing about with anticipation. I opened the screen door slightly and said, "Hello? Lisa?"

Lisa came to the door wearing nothing but a smile, a glass of red wine in her hand. Her hair was styled in a way I hadn't seen it before, away from her face and pulled back with a clip. She wore small gold stud earrings that complemented the gold chain around her neck. Her feet were bare, her toenails painted blue, and I noticed something even more intriguing. Her formerly lush pubic hair was trimmed down to a small patch, revealing her bare vulva.

In another context, a woman answering the door completely nude would imply that she was "open for business." This was not that context, however, and I reminded myself to behave as though she were fully clothed, keeping my hands and other appendages to myself.

"You look nice, Brian," said Lisa, and gave me a one-armed hug while still holding her wine glass.

"Thanks. As do you." And I meant it.

"Oh, this old thing? Had it for the past twenty-eight years. It's expanded in places, but I find it still suits me well."

I laughed. "That it does. Very well. I feel overdressed."

"You're not, but you can feel free to make yourself comfortable if you like." I shut the screen door behind me and Lisa led me into the kitchen. "I've got some chips and crab dip. Would you like a glass of wine?"

"Thanks, but I had better not. My last drinking experience nearly did me in and I'm trying to cut back."

"Okay. Understand. I'm sorry." Lisa looked hurt, then brightened. She opened the refrigerator and peered inside. "I've got some kind of seltzer in here."

"That's fine. Thanks."

Lisa handed me a seltzer. I popped and took a sip. It was cold, refreshing, and utterly tasteless. It wasn't gin and tonic, but it would suffice. Drinks were like props to me. I never knew what to do with my hands if I didn't have something contained in them, so I began to feel more at ease with my prop, non-alcoholic though it was. I had no idea what to expect from the evening but I hoped for more clarity in our relationship. Were we friends or becoming something more? Would I even go back to my own trailer tonight?

Lisa padded into her living room and plopped herself down on a pink towel that she had laid out. She propped her feet up on a low table and crossed her legs, then patted the couch beside her to indicate for me to sit down.

"So, how was your day, Brian?" she asked while twirling the stem of her nearly empty wine glass.

"Not bad. I went to see my grandma."

"Oh? How is she? Is she getting better?"

"Much better. Ornery as usual of course. Described the food as warm diarrhea."

Lisa scrunched up her nose and made a disgusted face. Somehow she still managed to look cute. "That's Clara. She cracks me up."

"Yup. I just can't stand nursing homes. The smells, the sounds, the hopelessness of it all. If I ever get to that point, just shoot me."

"Duly noted. I will remember that." She set her wine glass on the floor and pretended to write on her palm with the index finger of her other hand. "Shoot Brian when he gets old." She laughed.

A TV in the corner chattered away, airing some banal sitcom, but neither of us paid any attention. We conversed about the details of our day, mine in a nursing home and hers at a client's house, cleaning grout with a toothbrush.

"This client creeps me out, Brian. He's got money, because I've been over to his house twice now and I'm not cheap. Plus he's got a Land Rover in the driveway and his house is like a fucking mansion, but he's this overweight guy who breathes heavy and his eyes go two different directions, so I think he's staring at me but I'm not really sure. I doubt he's ever even been laid, despite all the money. Anyway, I'm naked, on my hands and knees cleaning this grout because unlike most of the girls who do this, I actually do a really good job of cleaning, and he's just standing there, breathing heavy and shit and looking at my bare ass."

"Isn't that the point though?"

"Is what the point?"

"Well, you clean houses naked because men like looking at you naked and that's why they pay extra. Otherwise, they'd have Merry Maids do the work or something, wearing clothes."

"I dunno. I guess, but have some respect. Like, back off a bit, you know? His face was so close to my ass I'm pretty sure he could

154

see what I had for breakfast. Anyway, I'm waiting to hear if I am getting into paramedic school this fall. I've made almost enough now with this cleaning job to pay my way through without having to work elsewhere and then I can just concentrate on school."

"Right on! Where would you go to school?"

"I applied to Tacoma Community College, so I'd move down there if I get in. I guess with the park being sold, it might be sooner rather than later. Then there's an online option as well that I'm looking into."

"Funny that you should mention that," I said. "My old department head just called me up and offered me employment as an online professor."

"Really?" said Lisa. "That's great news, Brian." She patted me on the knee. "I'd take a class from you. I'm sure it would be fascinating."

"Why would you need to take it online? I'd teach you in person."

"Naked?"

"In whatever mode of dress you wish," I replied. Now I was starting to get a bit giddy with the direction of the conversation. Parts of me were becoming even giddier than others.

I'd finished my seltzer and Lisa had finished her wine. She went back into the kitchen to fetch herself another glass and to get me another seltzer, And to retrieve the chips and dip. She plopped back in her spot, grabbed the remote, and flipped through what seemed like fifty channels before giving up.

"I'm bored of TV, you know? It's all so stupid. Hey, do you want to play Monopoly?"

"I was hoping you were going to ask if I wanted to play strip poker."

"Well, you've already won. I'm naked and you're not, so what's the point?"

"Very true. Sure, I'll play Monopoly."

She reached under the table and rummaged about in multiple stacks of board games, magazines, photo albums, and what looked to be archaic TV remote controls from televisions she presumably no longer owned. "Sorry. I'm not very organized," she said, before exclaiming "Aha!" and triumphantly retrieving Monopoly from somewhere in the middle of the mess.

Lisa sat cross-legged on the floor across from me, affording me an unobstructed view of her most intimate anatomy. Her inner right labia was pierced with a small ring that bore a bright blue ball. Without pubic hair, it was a lot easier to see, but I seemed to recall that when I had first seen her naked, her piercing had been silver.

I tried to find a way to compliment her on the jewelry without sounding like a pervert and making it seem obvious that I had been staring at her crotch. "I like your, um…piercing," I finally said.

"Oh thanks!" said Lisa, as she peered between her legs and took the blue ball between her first finger and thumb. She rolled it around between her fingers, stretching her lips slightly, as casually as if she were examining a ragged cuticle. "I like to accessorize sometimes. As you can see, I'm color-coordinated." She splayed out her fingers to show off her blue nail polish.

"Very nice," I said.

"Did my toenails too."

"I see that. And you've uh…you've shaved."

"Oh. Yeah. I get bored from time to time and shave the whole thing off. I like my pubic hair, but I guess it's kind of like a beard.

You know, guys can grow beards, mustaches, goatees, whatever, then shave them off. Well, I'm a girl and a nudist, so this is my own version of follicular creativity."

"I never really thought of that," I said. "I used to have this big professorial beard but my wife kept nagging me about it so I shaved it off."

"Really? You'd look good with a beard."

"Thanks. I'm not so sure about that."

"Anyway," continued Lisa. "For St. Patrick's Day one year, I had green nipple piercings, green nail polish, and I dyed my pubic hair green. It was awesome. Had a little more trouble with Independence Day. As it turned out, attempting to dye my pubes red, white, and blue didn't go so well."

I laughed. "That's something I'll have to try some day when I have a little more time under my belt as a nudist."

"Why not?" said Lisa. "It's all about having fun. Ready to play?"

Lisa set up the board and before long we were playing. She was the bank, of course, and soon she had bought up all railroads and several properties. Between generous gulps of wine and brief breaks to pee or fill up her wine glass, she gleefully set up houses and hotels, charged me exorbitant amounts of rent, and bought back most of my properties. I was having fun, though, and I could confidently say this was the first time I had ever played a board game with a naked girl. Lisa was visibly tipsier as the game progressed, eventually reaching a point at which she decided to put the game on hold.

"I can't concentrate on this anymore. Do you want to watch a movie?" she asked. "We can finish this game tomorrow."

She plopped back onto the couch and then flipped through Netflix before finding a particularly morbid crime documentary. "This work for you?" she asked. "I love true crime."

"Sure."

"I'm cold," she said.

"Can't imagine why."

She grabbed a fuzzy blanket from the back of the couch, spread it over both of our laps, and then scooted next to me. "You know how when you arrived you said you felt overdressed?"

"Um…yeah?"

"Well, you are."

"I can fix that," I said.

"Oh, so can I, Brian. So can I."

She worked at my belt while I fumbled with my zipper. Eventually I was able to unzip my pants. With glee, Lisa helped me to pull them off and tossed them on the floor, leaving me naked from the waist down. I felt the warmth of Lisa's right hand on my erection as she slowly stroked. I caressed the nape of her neck and kissed her on the mouth. Her lips were incredibly soft and tasted of Cabernet and strawberry lip balm. She arched, moaned, and thrust her tongue into my mouth. I fumbled with the buttons of my shirt before removing it as well, our lips still passionately locked. Lisa's right hand moved faster. It became too much and I had to gently push her hand away. I didn't want this to end too quickly.

My hands moved southward on her and then my tongue followed suit, kissing and licking her neck and then tracing a path down her belly. I tasted the subtle saltiness of her and smelled her lavender body wash. As my tongue explored the tender, smooth flesh of her inner thighs I felt the warmth from between her legs.

158

I gently parted her lips and inserted a finger. She was already incredibly wet. I stroked myself but only enough to maintain; it had been so long since I had had made love to anyone, much less a woman this beautiful. I didn't want it to come to an end prematurely.

I put my mouth on her and she pushed her pelvis towards me, moaning. My tongue explored every contour of her most intimate opening. Lisa grabbed the back of my head roughly and pulled me towards her. She was a woman who knew what she wanted. She moaned and then tensed, before gently pushing me away.

She pulled her feet onto the couch and laid on her back. I kissed her again before pulling her knees to her chest and entering her. I thrust slowly as I attempted to maintain control, but I was soon at the point of no return. I had to stop.

"Sorry," I said. "It's been a while."

Lisa giggled. "It's okay. Me too. No pressure." She looked stunning lying there, her long blond hair now free of its constraints and spread over the fabric of the couch. The blanket was somewhere on the floor or tangled at our feet.

When I regained my control, I started again. Lisa matched every thrust with her own. I steadied myself with my right hand while my left went under the small of her back. I felt her tight, muscular physique and the contractions of her back muscles as we got into synchrony.

Still inside of her, I cupped her small, supple breasts, encircling the nipples with my thumb and forefinger and felt them respond to my touch. I kissed behind her ear and down her neck before rising back up and thrusting once again. Her strong, athletic legs formed a viselike grip around my hips and her breath came in jagged bursts. Sweat formed on her lip and brow and her eyes rolled back. She moaned loudly and then we both came at once.

Wordlessly, Lisa turned to her side and closed her eyes, an ever-so-slight smile on her face. I got up, cleaned up, and urinated. When I returned, she had pulled the blanket over herself. She was already asleep. Quietly, I tucked in behind her, pulled the blanket over myself, and slept, Lisa's long blond hair caressing my chest, our breaths in synchrony, our legs intertwined. I honestly could not recall a time that I had had sex while completely sober, and it was better than anything. I was fully present with Lisa, my brain and other parts functioning perfectly.

We snoozed soundly for a while and then our post-coital slumber was interrupted by an awful screeching sound about an hour or so after we fell asleep. I shot up, nearly knocking Lisa to the floor. "What in the holy hell was that?" I asked.

Lisa slowly rose to a seated position, hair in eighteen different directions, with a blanket around her bare shoulders. She listened as a muffled female voice spoke in the darkness.

"Oh, that's just my fire radio," said Lisa. "It's a call for the north battalion. I'm east. Not that I'd go tonight anyway." She reached out, hit a button on a small device sitting on the coffee table, and laid back down. I was amazed at how something so small could make such a terrific racket.

"How do you get any decent sleep with all that noise?" I asked.

"Hmmm. Sometimes I don't. Depends on the night. Goodnight." She was back to softly snoring in less than a minute. It took me a bit longer to get back to sleep myself.

I awoke several hours later to the smell of freshly brewed coffee and the glint of morning sunlight passing through the blinds. I thought I detected a hint of bacon as well. Lisa was no longer beside me on the couch. I opened my eyes briefly, peered around, and closed them again. No headache. No cottonmouth. There were definitely benefits of not drinking alcohol the night before.

I did need to urinate though, so I cast off the blanket and stood up. I had some significant "morning wood" going on. Lisa was standing in the small kitchen, clad in shorts and T-shirt with bare feet. Her hair was up in a messy bun.

"Good morning, Brian," she said from the kitchen. "Coffee?"

"Yes, please."

I figured I needn't worry about my morning erection flopping about as I headed to the bathroom. We'd already crossed that threshold. I also saw no need to dress immediately, though I was somewhat puzzled that she felt compelled to, especially after what we'd experienced together the previous night.

After forcing my turgid penis downwards and managing somehow to avoid spraying urine all over the curtains and walls, I washed my hands and walked back into the kitchen, my member slowly assuming a more comfortable droop.

"How do you take your coffee?" asked Lisa.

"Strong and bitter, just like my ex-wife."

She laughed. "Okay, then black, I take it." She poured a mug and handed it to me. "How did you sleep?"

"Aside from Armageddon occurring at some ungodly hour last night, I slept very well, thanks. You?"

"Yeah, sorry about my fire radio. Forgot to turn it off. I slept like a rock."

I sipped my coffee while Lisa laid bacon out on paper towels. In another pan, she was scrambling eggs with cheese. "You like green peppers? I was going to put some in."

"Sure. Sounds great."

161

Lisa handed me a plate of bacon and eggs and we sat down to eat, our roles reversed from last night, Lisa clothed and me naked. I remembered the first cardinal rule of nudism, always put down a towel to sit on.

"What's on your agenda today?" asked Lisa.

"Substitute lecturing today at eleven. Oh no. Where's my phone?" I located my pants, still crumpled up on the floor where I had discarded them in the throes of passion. I located my phone in a front pocket. The display read 9:12. I also noticed that I had a new voice mail and figured I would wait until later to retrieve it. "Yeah, I should get going pretty soon."

We chatted a little bit longer, but I couldn't help but notice some subtle changes in Lisa's demeanor since last night. A woman who loved to be naked was uncharacteristically dressed. She didn't exactly avoid eye contact entirely, but did avert her eyes a few times across the table, and seemed generally subdued, but not unfriendly. Oddly, there was no talk of the festivities we had engaged in the previous night, though I wasn't sure what I expected from her anyway. A high five?

I dressed and thanked Lisa for breakfast. She gave me a hug and a kiss on the cheek before I left to go back to Grandma's trailer. "I'll give you a call later," she said, and I hoped she meant it.

I dashed out the door in time to grab a quick shower at Grandma's trailer, threw on some clothing that made me look somewhat professorial, and jetted off to the college, just barely squeaking on time for lecture.

The guest lecture was a subject with which I was well-versed, the endocrine system. For fifty-five minutes, I expounded on the hypothalamic-pituitary axis, the adrenal cortex and medulla, and a survey of endocrine diseases and conditions, including Waterhouse-Friderichson syndrome, Addison's disease, and thyrotoxicosis. Since it was a survey course and more academic than clinical, I took the glazed eyes of some of those in the front row as a clue that I should probably move on to other related subjects, rather than belabor every sign and symptom. I would have become a physician but as I have discovered, I am no help at all in an actual emergency. I have fainted at the sight of my own blood.

After class, I returned home, flicked on the television, and then checked my phone. I was disappointed to see that Lisa hadn't called while I was out but reminded myself that she had a busy life, probably friends to see, work to do, etc. As I flipped aimlessly through Facebook and read emails that consisted mainly of ads for penis enlargement pills, something I've never needed, I remembered that I hadn't checked my voice mail.

The message, to my great chagrin, was from my estranged wife, stating that she was serving me with papers and that it was her intention to be awarded half of my retirement to date, since we had been married ten years. After this uplifting little bit of news, I decided to reward myself by opening the stack of bills that had been accumulating dust on the counter for over a week. I had a morbid fear of bills, even more so now that my ability to pay them had become rather compromised.

Contained in the pile of bills was a past due notice from one credit card company—my limit was already exceeded, a bill from another credit card company that was due in two days, my car payment, and a maintenance bill from an apartment I no longer lived in, kindly billed to me by my lovely soon-to-be ex-wife.

I was beginning to get a bit of a headache. I sauntered into the kitchen, telling myself I was going to get a glass of water but somehow, inexplicably, found myself bent down, peering into the liquor cabinet, staring at a half-empty bottle of gin.

I wasted a good ten minutes of my afternoon staring at, then removing the bottle of gin, having a pointless conversation with it, walking away, coming back, unscrewing the top, going so far as to tip it back towards my lips, then tipping it towards the sink, rethinking my plan, screwing the top back on, and walking away again. If ever I wanted a drink, it was now. And Lisa still hadn't called. Or texted. Or stopped by. Maybe I should walk over there? No. Too desperate.

Frustrated in more ways than one, I grabbed a Sprite from the fridge, plopped myself on the couch, and watched the news until dinner, which consisted of one of Grandma's TV dinners and a small carton of yogurt. Both were unappetizing. After checking my phone about a dozen more times, I fell asleep on the couch and didn't wake up until early the next morning.

An Offer

Trudging along Deep Valley's inner loop at eight o'clock in the morning, getting some fresh air, a steaming mug of coffee in my hands, moccasins crunching along in the gravel, when Security Bob, in his favorite mode of transport, drove past me in his golf cart and came to a stop immediately ahead of me in a cloud of dust. He waited for me to catch up before leaning out and taking a drag off his cigarette.

"Hey," he said, with the smoking butt held betwixt his thumb and forefinger. "Just got done talking to Earl. He's got an offer on the park."

"Hmmm. That was quick. Hasn't it only been on the market for a week?"

"Yeah. Something like that. Earl says it's some preacher with a lot of money. Fella by the name of Dale Parkhurst, runs a church in Concrete. You know him, by chance?"

"I do not." My increasingly tanned behind had not darkened the door of a church since I was a kid growing up in California.

"Well anyway," continued Bob. "He's buying it with an inheritance he has from his brother, William, who was a big shot real estate developer in the area. Bit of an arrogant asshole. Died a couple years back. Lung cancer." Bob took a last drag on his cigarette before squashing the butt in a Coke can he kept in a holder on the dash and I really questioned if he understood the irony of what he had just said.

"Interesting. How long until we know if Earl accepts?"

"Should be within just a few days."

"And how long until we all have to move out?"

"That I don't know. I imagine it will be stipulated by the buyer."

"What did you say his name was again?"

"Reverend Dale Parkhurst."

Bob zoomed off again, disappearing in a cloud of dust that inevitably settled on to my sweatpants. I coughed, dusted myself off, and continued on my walk around the park. When my coffee had gone from lukewarm to cold, I decided that I had achieved my exercise quota for the day. I headed back to Grandma's trailer.

I stewed for quite some time before, on a hunch, I decided to make my way to the office and do some research. Nobody was there, so I used my own key to unlock the door, flipped on the lights, and began searching for the Book of Shame.

Eventually I located it, underneath a stack of magazines. I flipped through the pages, feeling a sense of guilt as though I were delving into something very private, but then reminded myself that it was not only my right, but my responsibility as president to ensure that the park was safe from creepy folks. There were quite a few names there, with incident reports attached, dating all the way back to nearly the beginning of the club.

There were references to a few individuals who had been booted for intoxication and flagrant disregard for the social mores of the community. One page referred to a fellow who was found to be photographing visitors to the park and when he was confronted he flipped the bird to one of the senior club members. It didn't end well for him. Another page elucidated the 86'ing of an elderly man who visited one day and failed to completely undress, yet stood in the shadows with his pants unzipped, pleasuring himself while staring at a couple sunbathing on the lawn.

Then I got a surprise. Page thirty-two of the Book of Shame referred to an individual known as Dale Parkhurst with a date of birth of November 2, 1953. An incident report was attached which read, "Complainant: Dolores Eisenberg. Complainant states she encountered subject when she exited the pool restroom. Subject was partially dressed, had an erection, and was masturbating in the vicinity of a young male (age approximately eight to twelve) who was visiting the park with his parents and sister. The young male was unaware that the subject in question was watching him. Dolores confronted the subject, who became angry and argumentative. He was then asked to leave the grounds. The American Association of Nude Recreation was also contacted. Subject is banned from this establishment."

I was stunned. If I wasn't mistaken, the man in question was the potential buyer of Deep Valley Nudist Park's property, and a man of the cloth at that! Knowing this information, I couldn't let the purchase go through.

COFFEE WITH LISA

Four days after our tryst, Lisa finally rang me up. She said that she was sorry that she hadn't been in contact but that she wanted to talk to me. We agreed to meet at a coffee shop in Downtown Concrete the following morning.

At around nine o'clock, I pulled into Lavon's Café off Highway 20. It was a charming little place and very busy for such a small town. Behind the cash register stood a weathered, world-weary woman with no teeth, no make-up, and gray hair tied back with a green rubber band. She did smile broadly though when I walked in, handed me a menu, and seated me at a table.

Lisa texted me to say that she was running just a little bit late, so I ordered a cup of black coffee and leaned back in my chair to observe the goings-on. The café walls featured numerous black-and-white photographs depicting logging activities from the earlier part of the last century, most of them askew—memories of the logging boom that had long since reached its apex and declined rapidly, leaving so many upriver folks out of work. The woman at the counter looked like she had lived through a couple of centuries herself.

In the center of the room sat four late middle-aged women, all of whom were rather plump as well as quite loud. An elderly man with a long gray beard tried to read his newspaper at a corner table and kept looking up at them with annoyance. The woman at the counter continued to look harried as she distributed menus, rang up sales, and cleaned up tables. It appeared she was the only one actually working.

Lisa arrived a few minutes later. The woman at the counter smiled and then spread her arms out and hugged Lisa. They chatted for a few seconds and then Lisa pointed towards my table. The other woman nodded. Then Lisa walked over to me and gave me a hug.

"Do you mind if we move?" she asked. "I'd just like a little more privacy."

"Sure," I said.

We moved to a little corner table. Lisa ordered a twenty-ounce hazelnut latte and a Danish. She placed her right hand on my left and looked me in the eye. "How are you, Brian?"

"I'm well, thanks. You're very popular around here."

"Oh, yeah. I've been coming here for years. Lavon is an old friend of mine. Salt of the earth, you know? She's owned this shop for over twenty years, I think. I don't think she's ever left Concrete. She's just the sweetest person."

"She seems very nice."

I noticed that the four stout women at the adjacent table had begun casting glances in our direction and then leaning their heads forward in a conspiratorial manner, whispering amongst themselves.

"What's their issue?" I asked. "Do you know them too?"

"Ugh," replied Lisa. "Unfortunately, I do. That's the Cliterati."

I laughed out loud. "What? The Cliterati?"

"They are all members of that Non-denominational Church here in town. They've always got their noses in the air, think their shit don't stink, look down on everyone. You know, those kind of people."

"And they know you?"

"The Cliterati know everybody. I'm not sure how, but they knew my parents, and also knew they were members of Deep Valley, so obviously they were sinners of the worst kind. I was their daughter, so I'm pretty much damned to Hell as well!" Lisa laughed.

"They sound delightful."

"Right. Absolutely no redeeming qualities at all, except in their own fucked up universe. They really believe that they are the moral conscience of the community. And poor Lavon has to put up with their shit every week."

Lisa's coffee and Danish arrived. She took a big gulp of her coffee. "So," she said. "I wanted to talk to you about, you know, the other night."

My heart sank in my chest. "Okay?"

"I don't want you to think I'm ignoring you, "Lisa began. "It's just…"

"Yes?"

"Okay, I picked this place because if we were back at my trailer or your trailer, things might get out of hand."

Lisa read the disappointment on my face and grabbed both of my hands in hers. She looked into my eyes. "I don't regret what happened at all," she said. "And it was really nice waking up with you in the morning. I just don't want you to get the wrong idea."

Well, that was definitely not what I wanted to hear. Why had I built up a relationship in my head that didn't exist in reality?

"Remember when I told you that I don't date?" I nodded. "I'm going to tell you something really personal. I've been married before."

"Okay."

"I married my high school sweetheart. He worked at Janicki Industries on the night shift. One night we got into a knockout, drag out argument about some little minx he'd been friendly to at work. I thought there was more to it, and he insisted there wasn't. He got really drunk and then left, said I didn't trust him and he couldn't handle that. Well, two hours later, I get a call from State Patrol that he's dead. He slammed into a telephone pole on Fruitdale Road. I still have no idea where he was going. I've blamed myself for his death ever since."

"I'm so sorry," I said. I was at a loss for words.

"I like you, Brian," Lisa said. "I just want to take it slow, and I don't want you to feel like you're competing with a dead man."

"I understand," I said. "I'm still officially married, so I guess I need to take it slow as well."

"Well, there's that little hurdle as well. How is that process going, by the way?"

"Got served with divorce papers the other day. She's going after my retirement, among other things. At least we didn't own a house together."

"That sucks. It really does." Lisa once again put her hand, warmed by her coffee cup, on top of mine. "I'm sorry."

"A whole lot of sorrys going around," I said. Lisa laughed.

"You know what I'm really sorry about?" I continued. "The Park has a potential buyer. A Dale Parkhurst?"

"What? Seriously? That guy's a huge douchebag."

"Oh, you know him?"

"Unfortunately, I do." She nodded towards the Cliterati. "He leads their church. Runs his mouth around town about what a bunch of moral degenerates we all are at Deep Valley. Believe me, I've got nothing against religion. I grew up Lutheran. But when you use your religion as a weapon? Ugh."

"Well the truly disturbing thing," I said, "and I shouldn't be telling you this..." Lisa leaned in. I'd begun to realize she loved juicy gossip. "Is that Dale Parkhurst has already been banned from Deep Valley for inappropriate sexual activity."

"Seriously? No shit?" Lisa clapped a hand to her mouth. "Oops." She cast a glance at the Cliterati, one or two of whom glared back. "Better keep my voice down or these bitches will make it their mission to make my life a living Hell."

"Lisa, we can't let that happen. We can't let a creep buy the park."

"What does it matter? It won't once he owns the place, whether he's been banned or not. We'll all be out on our bare asses anyway."

"True, but it still irritates me. It seems so vindictive to me, like he's avenging his lifetime ban from the park by making sure that he wins in the end."

"Yeah. I hate hypocrites."

Before I could respond, there was a loud screeching sound from Lisa's general direction. Everyone in the café turned to look. I recognized the screeching as the same sound that had awoken me from a dead sleep days ago at Lisa's place.

"Damn, Lisa. Doesn't that thing have a vibrate function?"

"Oh it does. I just forget to set it that way." She grabbed the pager from her hip, turned it down, and held it to her ear.

"Shit!" she said. "It's CPR in progress at Deep Valley!" She took a final slurp from her coffee and banged the cup down. "Sorry. Gotta go. I'll call you." Then she was out the door and running to her car. A minute later, through the window, I saw her truck roaring past. It looked like she had green flashing lights in the truck's grill.

I finished my coffee and Lisa's half-eaten Danish as well. I was not one to let food go to waste. Then I headed out the door and drove back to the park. I was curious about who it was that had a medical emergency.

When I arrived back at Grandma's trailer, I had a bit of a PTSD moment, recalling Grandma's fall. The same emergency vehicles were there, some in front of Grandma's trailer and others in front of Dolores's. In addition, there was a Sheriff's Office patrol vehicle parked slightly to the north. Predictably, Security Bob's golf cart was there as well, amber roof light flickering. Lisa's truck was parked just ahead of it. I spotted several fire volunteers milling about in Dolores's yard but couldn't make out much else. None of them seemed to be in any hurry. I thought that could either be a good sign or a very bad one.

Not wanting to stand and stare, as were four or five other naked people and their dog, I walked into my trailer. However, I did open the blinds to see the action from afar. If I was going to be a lookie-loo, I would be a subtle lookie-loo.

After a few minutes, I noticed vehicles beginning to leave, turning off their reds lights and pulling away slowly, first the volunteer rigs and then the medic unit. Finally, Lisa's truck and the Sheriff's vehicle were the only two to remain.

I heard a knock on my door and answered it to find Lisa standing on my doorstep. Since she had left the coffee shop, she had thrown on a rather shapeless blue quarter-zip sweatshirt emblazoned with a fire department logo.

"What happened?" I asked.

"Dolores passed away."

"Oh no! How? Come in."

"Bob was doing his rounds and found her collapsed in her garden. Still had her gardening gloves on and a spade in one hand. I think she had a stroke."

I gave Lisa a long hug. When she pulled away, I noticed that her eyes were filled with tears. She wiped them away with the back of her hand.

"She wasn't at all well," said Lisa. "She was diabetic and had high blood pressure. I knew she couldn't stay at Deep Valley much longer with her health the way it was, but I never expected it so soon, you know." Lisa sat on the couch and sighed. "Well, at least she died doing what she loved, gardening naked in the sun."

"There's a lot to be said for that." I put my arm around her. We talked for a while about Dolores and Lisa's memories of the other old-timers who had since passed away. Deep Valley was becoming more of a retirement community where clothing was optional. Not much new blood came in after the old ones either died or moved to more conventional retirement communities.

I brewed a pot of coffee and we sat and talked for some time, enjoying each other's company despite the sad occasion. After about an hour, a white van slowly pulled up to Dolores's trailer. I went to the window to get a closer look. Written on the passenger door of the van was "Hirsch Chapel of Bellingham." Underneath the lettering was a Star of David.

"Well," I said. "That's the funeral home, I guess."

"Yeah," said Lisa. "Can you close the blinds please, Brian? I don't want to see them take her away."

POSTMORTEM

The mood was profoundly somber around Deep Valley the next day. I noticed also that some of the "always nude" people had taken to wearing clothes. I asked Lisa about that and she said that it seemed weird but that she felt the same way. "Nudity is about joy. This is not a joyful occasion," she had said. For a couple days she took to wearing her sundress or shorts and a T-shirt but after a while, the clothes came back off again for her and for the majority of Deep Valley attendees.

The weekend after Dolores's death, we held a little memorial for her at Deep Valley. Her wishes, filed years earlier with Hirsch Chapel, were for no public service, but we arranged our own. It seemed only right that such a pillar of the community be honored in some way. Ever the contrarian, she had chosen to be cremated instead of buried as her Jewish faith would dictate. Her ashes had been sent to a sister in Florida. Dave the Hippie was an ordained minister in some obscure religion and led the service, held in the clubhouse and attended by almost every member of Deep Valley. At the front of the room was a photograph of Dolores at the last Halloween Party, beaming broadly. She had come as a pumpkin, and the only things she needed to do were to paint her body orange and wear a green hat that resembled a stem. Dolores had appeared happy, living in the moment as she always did. Dave had trimmed his beard for the occasion, pulled back his long hair, and wore a button-up shirt and pants. Come to think of it, it was the first time I had ever seen him with clothes on.

Dave began the service by saying, "Dolores didn't die with her boots on, but she wouldn't have wanted to. She passed away suddenly but peacefully, halfway through weeding her flower bed, wearing nothing but a pair of gardening gloves and cheap plastic clogs. She took her last breath holding the hand of her long-time friend Bob Haussmann, her eyes closed, and her head resting gently on a giant dandelion that she had undoubtedly been planning to murder." There was some quiet laughter at this point to lessen the somber mood. Members exchanged anecdotes and the service was concluded with a toast to Dolores. Shot glasses of Cabernet were passed around; I toasted Dolores with a shot of water. We were as different as could be, but in the end we were family. Dave announced plans to place a memorial bench in front of Dolores's trailer, where old and weary members could pause and rest on their way to and from their destinations.

Taking a Stand

The council met in executive session at the clubhouse the following weekend and by that time the news of the park's imminent sale to Reverend Parkhurst had already spread like wildfire. Most didn't know who he was, but those that did didn't have many accolades for him. He was known locally as a zealot, a busybody, and a generally intolerant boozehound who would cover up his own weaknesses and inadequacies by pointing out those of others.

Nonetheless, he was about to be the new owner of the land on which Deep Valley was built, so none of that really mattered. The dominant rumor flying around the community was that he was planning to tear down the existing structures and put in condominiums, an odd choice for a predominantly rural area. Despite the apparent inevitability of the sale, the whole situation irked me, and I was about to bring up my concerns with my fellow council members.

I walked naked to the council meeting as had become my custom, towel slung over my back, coffee mug in my left hand, uncharacteristically absent the alcohol. The first few dry days were awfully tough, but it was beginning to ease up. I may have gotten over the first hurdle, but my race to sobriety was far from over.

When I walked through the doors, I saw the table set up with Gunter and Judy already seated. Dolores's name plate still sat in front of her empty chair, much like my grandmother's had before I took over. Somebody had placed her favorite coffee cup there and stuck a dandelion in it—a simple but poignant gesture, and though I hardly had the chance to get to know Dolores, it still put a lump in my throat. The club was shrinking, slowly but agonizingly ebbing away with the aging and death of its core members. It made me sad, but I wasn't going to let it go without a fight, more for my grandmother and the old-timers than for myself.

Gunter distributed a copy of the agenda, which took up no more than a quarter of a page. This was going to be a short meeting. Judy had temporarily taken over treasurer duties in the wake of Dolores's demise and gave a rather pitiable accounting of the club's financial situation. After some discussion on the last events to be held this year, Gunter turned to me and asked me if I had anything to add.

I cleared my throat and took a swig of my coffee. "As you all know, we are in our last couple of months as a club and that the property is being sold to an individual known as Rev. Dale Parkhurst. Well, what you might not know is that I happened upon the Book of Shame and found his name in it."

Judy and Gunter's jaws dropped. "What?" Judy asked.

"He has received a lifetime ban from this property for inappropriate sexual behavior on the grounds. I know that once he owns the property he can do what he wants with it, but I find the idea of selling the property to a hypocrite and a pervert to be particularly repugnant. I'd like to think that if my grandmother were here, she would be opposed as well and probably use more color-ful language to get her point across."

Gunter chuckled at that last sentence. "That is certainly inter-esting news and I will mention it to Mr. White. I will say, though, that it may fall on deaf ears. Mr. White needs to consider first his financial situation and what makes sense from that standpoint. I do appreciate your input though, Brian." Gunter's voice then changed to a stern, fatherly tone. "I would be very careful though, about referring to a potential buyer as a "pervert" or anything of the like. This is a very small community and I refer to both the nudist community and Eastern Skagit County. I do appreciate your input though, and I find the information concerning."

"Thank you and I apologize for referring to him the way I did. I don't know him. I just feel it might not make sense to take the first offer that comes to the table. The sale of the park to…to such an individual seems an insult to you, Judy, my grandmother, Dolores…"

Judy said, "We hear you, Brian, and we will forward your con-cern to Earl White." Gunter looked dejected.

That evening, I sat on the couch and worried. I had spread my towel out and thrown a blanket over my lap because the days were getting shorter and it was starting to get colder earlier. My feet were ice cubes, so I donned a pair of wool socks but nothing else. I opened a can of Sprite, poured it over ice, pretended I was drink-ing alcohol, and felt generally dissatisfied and bored. I worried about my grandmother and whether she would ever come home, I worried about the future of my career—if there was one—and I worried that I'd blown things with Lisa because I'd slept with her too soon. I checked my phone neurotically, each time disap-pointed that she hadn't called or texted. After an unproductive hour or two of finding nothing of entertainment value on television, I opened my laptop and began searching for a new place to live, hopefully one that would accommodate Grandma as well. There wasn't much in Skagit County for rent and what narrowed the search even more was that, for Grandma's sake, it needed to be on the first floor and have no stairs. Everything was ridiculously overpriced. After some fruitless searching, I closed my laptop again. I sauntered back into the kitchen, opened up the liquor cabinet and stared at the bottle of gin again. Then I reminded myself of my promise not to drink. Though it pained me greatly to say goodbye to a friend, I unscrewed the cap and poured it down the drain. Tomorrow morning I would teach lab. I needed a good night of sleep.

Lying in bed in the silence, I felt very lonely. I checked the phone one last time to see if Lisa had called. She hadn't. Eventually, I was able to turn my brain off and sleep.

I awoke after seven hours of solid sleep, uninterrupted by my usual alcohol-induced three a.m. insomnia. I shaved, showered, remembered to put on pants, and headed to the college.

Lab went well. The students were eager to learn and asked lots of questions. I was helping to prepare them for the final histology examination of summer quarter and had set out tissue samples from various parts of the mammalian body that they needed to identify under microscopes. There were squamous skin cells, ciliated columnar cells from the respiratory tract, and cuboidal cells from the bladder among others.

On my way home, my phone rang. I took a quick glance at the caller ID and saw that it was from Lisa. My heart leaped and I rushed to answer it, nearly driving off the road in the process.

I swerved back into my lane and put Lisa on speakerphone. "Hey Lisa, what's up?"

"Nothing. Just finished a job and I've got nothing going on for a few days. Do you feel like getting out of town with me?"

"Where? For how long?"

"I don't know. I just need to get outta here for a while, see where my truck takes me. Maybe three or four days?"

"Okay. I've got to see if I can switch things around at work and get some time off. When were you thinking of leaving?"

"Tomorrow morning. I'm going to hitch up my trailer and take my house with me. Not even sure I'm going to return."

ROAD TRIP

Lisa and I agreed to meet the following morning at seven at her trailer. I had packed some toiletries and clothing for a trip to God knows where. Spontaneity was not my strong suit, but I was willing to go where the adventure took me if it was with Lisa. When I met her at the trailer, she had already hitched it up to her truck and the engine was idling. She certainly didn't waste any time. When I first approached, I didn't see her, then I spotted her crouched down behind her truck, wearing nothing but a pair of hiking boots and a baseball cap, hooking up her taillights and chains.

She stood. "Hey Brian!" She gave me a warm, full-body hug with the exception of her hands. "Sorry. My hands are greasy," she said. "Let me just wash them and we can be on our way. Got your stuff?"

I loaded my bags into the cab of the pickup. Lisa washed her hands in the trailer, got into the driver's seat and shut the door. "Packing for a trip is easy when you bring your house with you!" she said. "I feel like a snail, with my home on my back."

"Thankfully, you don't physically resemble a snail," I quipped.

I closed the passenger door after moving a pile of food wrappers and paperwork off the seat. Everything was an adventure with Lisa, and I had no idea what to expect from our impromptu road trip.

She slowly pulled away from her campsite, glancing frequently in the mirrors to make sure that her trailer was free of any obstructions. All that remained at her lot were a couple of camp chairs and a barbecue that looked to have seen better days.

She had driven past the office and down the gravel road, and was about to turn onto Highway 20 when she suddenly stopped and abruptly put the truck in park. "Shit!" she shouted, and then began laughing. "Know what I forgot?" It took me a few seconds before I realized it myself. "Clothes! I'm still naked!" Honestly, I was so used to seeing Lisa naked that it didn't even dawn on me that we were about to leave our clothing-optional sanctuary and venture out into the real world. We were within feet of Highway 20. A car whizzed by every few seconds.

"Dammit. I'm not putting it in reverse with the fifth wheel attached," Lisa said. "I'd just drive naked but everyone can see my tits."

"Is that such a bad thing?" I asked with a smirk.

"Not if it gets me pulled over," Lisa said.

"I'm sure you'd make some Highway Patrolman's day."

I could see the wheels turning in Lisa's head. "To Hell with it," she said. "I'm just going to have to make a dash for it." Lisa flung open her door just as a car passed. She stepped out, naked but for her boots and hat. Unfortunately the configuration of the fifth wheel meant she was only able to access the door and thus her clothing from the passenger's side of the trailer. She crossed in front of her truck just as an eighteen-wheeler whizzed by. The driver blasted his horn. Lisa smiled and waved as she ran back to her trailer.

She returned a minute or so later, taking her time on the return trip, wearing tiny shorts and a T-shirt. She got in, closed the door, and put the rig into drive before pulling out onto Highway 20.

"Well, you made that trucker's day," I said. "I think the horn blast said it all."

Lisa giggled. I glanced over and it was very obvious she wasn't wearing a bra. Her nipples were erect, tenting the thin fabric of her shirt. Her face was flushed. "That was kind of a rush," she said. "I'm a bit of an exhibitionist at heart, but I try not to offend anybody."

"Oh trust me," I said. "You didn't offend that trucker one bit."

"You think?" said Lisa. "I mean I guess it's not all that weird. There's that sign right at the end of the road that says Deep Valley Nudist Park."

"Yeah," I said. "Pretty sure he wasn't looking at the sign."

We drove on for a couple of minutes before I decided to pipe up again. "So, where are we headed?"

"That's a dumb question. Don't you know me by now? I have no idea where we are headed. No idea at all. Just sit back and enjoy."

Lisa cracked her window open to let in the breeze. The weather was beautiful and the sun was just rising over the hills as we traversed the last couple of miles to Interstate 5. The motor hummed and I could just barely hear the radio, tuned to a country station, turned down to an almost inaudible level. I wondered which direction Lisa would turn. She chose to head south.

Silence dominated the trip for at least half an hour, but it was a companionable silence. The seats were comfortable, the breeze felt amazing, and I had a beautiful woman seated beside me. All that I needed was a cup of coffee in my hand.

Finally, Lisa broke the silence. "So, Brian…"

"Yes?"

"I asked you to come along with me because…"

"Because?"

"I've been doing some thinking. The sale of the park is really bumming me out. I needed to get away and, well…I felt that you and I share something really special. I know I'm skittish, but I felt like we needed to get out of the context of the park to really get to know each other."

"I appreciate that."

"And…I'd really like to get to know you better."

"As would I."

"What was your childhood like? Who were your friends as a kid? What are your parents like?"

"Well, I grew up in Northern California," I said. "I didn't have many friends. I was very studious, a bit of a nerd, if you will. I never did sports. I was a band geek and in math club. My parents, God bless them, tried to get me to play sports, but I just plain sucked. Kept making goals for the opposite team, stared off into space at baseball when I could have made the catch…"

Lisa laughed. "I figured as much. And your parents?"

"Still together after forty years. They live in Oregon, actually, Milwaukie. Yours?"

"Still together as well," said Lisa. "I grew up in Skagit County. My parents and I spent the weekends at Deep Valley and eventually we got our own lot. We've got our original fifth wheel trailing behind us now. I guess I still live there because of a lack of motivation."

"How so?" I asked.

"After I graduated high school, I had no particular direction. I waitressed, I worked in a car dealership, I tried to go to college..."

"Tried to go to college?"

"I figured it was the thing to do, but I had no interest or aptitude for any of the classes I took, so I dropped out. Finally, a few years back, I got involved in the fire department, and I've been hooked ever since."

"What do you like best about the fire department?" I asked.

"The firefighting is fun, but we don't get to do it very often. I guess I was always more interested in emergency medicine. It's why I became an EMT. I love anatomy and I pick it up really easily."

"Now you're speaking my language. I went to many years of school to learn all I could about anatomy and physiology."

"I know. That's so cool. I need to pick your brain sometime. Hey, with your knowledge and experience, have you ever thought of becoming an EMT or volunteering for the fire district?"

"No, Lisa, though I appreciate your apparent confidence in me. I've come to realize that I'm absolutely no help at all in a real emergency."

"Oh, come on," said Lisa. "You're a doctor!"

"I'm an academic. I have a PhD, not an MD. Would you like to know what happened the last time I came upon an actual emergency? I was on a flight to Chicago for a conference and the flight attendant asked if there was a doctor on board. Without thinking and I suppose with a misguided sense of duty, I approached the flight attendant and told her that I was a doctor. There was this guy in first class that said he couldn't breathe; he was flailing around and breathing really fast. Well, I thought he was hyperventilating, so I gave him a paper bag to breathe into."

"And how did that work for you?"

"Not good. Not good. Turns out he was having an asthma attack."

"So what happened with him?"

"He lived, despite my effort. A doctor from China who didn't speak any English finally showed up, shoved me aside, gave the guy oxygen, and helped him find his inhaler. If it weren't for him, things might have been a whole lot worse."

I looked over at Lisa after I had finished my story and saw that she was biting her lip, trying not to laugh. "What's so funny? My patient almost died!"

"Oh, Brian. That's a great story. Maybe you shouldn't be an EMT. I guess you're book-smart and I'm street-smart. That's why we make a good team."

"Yeah," I said. "I guess you're right."

We stopped in Olympia to refuel. Adjacent to the gas station was a café where we refueled our bodies after refueling Lisa's truck. As luck would have it, they served breakfast all day so we feasted on pancakes, eggs, bacon, and slugged down cup after cup of coffee. We were so busy wolfing down our food, we didn't speak to each other much. When Lisa left to use the bathroom, I grabbed the bill.

"Got an idea," said Lisa. "Your parents live in Milwaukie, yeah?" Before giving me the opportunity to answer, she said, "There's a nude beach along the Columbia River that I've always wanted to visit. Would you like to go there today and then visit your parents tonight?"

"Sounds great. I'll see what they are doing this evening."

While Lisa pulled back onto the interstate, I called my parents. They were surprised and happy to hear from me, and even more excited at the prospect of meeting the new lady in my life. We tentatively agreed to meet at a local restaurant at seven that night.

"So where's this nude beach?"

"It's called Collins Beach, on Sauvie Island," said Lisa. "I'm excited to go because it's a sandy beach with fresh water, and I've never been to a beach like that before."

After about two hours, we crossed the Sauvie Island Bridge. We stopped at the Cracker Barrel store just on the other side of the bridge and obtained supplies for our day at the beach, sunscreen, Slim Jims, ice, pre-packaged sandwiches, beer for Lisa and bottled water for me. Lisa had a cooler in the fifth wheel, and we packed it full.

Once we got back into the truck and underway, Lisa said, "I forgot something."

"What's that?"

"How am I going to park this thing?"

Luckily, we happened upon a small trailer park that had vacancy. I paid the fee for the day and Lisa expertly backed the fifth wheel into the spot before disconnecting it so we could continue to the beach. "Our little home away from home," she said.

Sans trailer, we continued on to the beach. Lisa rolled up her windows as the gravel road was extremely dusty. Finally we pulled in to a spot alongside multiple dust-covered cars. Lisa poured a beer into a large, ice-filled plastic bottle and then strategically hid the rest of the beer in a backpack. "I've heard you aren't supposed

189

to drink here," she said. "You may have to drive back if I get a little buzzed."

I grabbed the cooler full of water and snacks out of the back of the truck. Lisa grabbed a bag containing towels and sunscreen, then cast a furtive glance in both directions before shucking her clothes and throwing them in the truck. I had begun to realize that part of Lisa's attraction to nudism was the thrill she got from being almost caught naked in public but not quite. I began to wonder if she had conveniently "forgotten" to put on clothes before we had left the park.

We walked the narrow path towards the beach. Once we got beyond the trees, the view opened up, revealing the full expanse of the shore. Scores of deeply tanned sun enthusiasts lined the sand, reclining on towels, cavorting in the water, or playing volleyball.

"Awesome!" said Lisa. "Hang on a sec. I need to water a plant." She stepped slightly off-trail, hands on hips, then thrust her pelvis forward, spread her legs, and released a bright amber torrent of recycled coffee onto the beige sand, splattering her bare feet. "See! Who says you have to be a man to pee standing up? I've been practicing!"

An elderly man, who seemed to be making his way back to his towel from a dip in the water, paused in his tracks, stared for a few seconds in Lisa's direction, and then continued his slow trudge back to his towel. Lisa urinated for nearly a full minute, the stream finally ebbing to a dribble. She performed her customary dance to shake off the final drops and continued on.

"I'm truly impressed with your many talents, Lisa," I said, "but do you think you might be a little more subtle about it?"

"Nah. I don't care." Lisa shrugged, grinned, waggled her tight butt for my benefit, and kept on walking.

She found a suitable spot and first spread out my towel and then hers. Then she pulled out her clandestine alcohol container, took a generous gulp, and then set about rubbing sunscreen on her face, breasts, and belly. "Can you get my back?" she asked.

Of course I could. What a silly question. I squirted sunscreen onto my palm, rubbed my hands together, and massaged it into Lisa's skin, first her shoulders, then her back, and finally her waist, paying particular attention to her supple buttocks. My hand may have even ventured elsewhere for a few seconds.

"That's enough," said Lisa, giggling. "You're going to get us in trouble."

I got naked and had to sit down on the towel for a minute while I waited for certain parts of my anatomy to behave.

"Would you like to go for a walk?" said Lisa. "All that time in the truck has got me needing to stretch my legs."

We took a stroll down the beach. She clutched her undercover beer, taking frequent gulps from it. I brought with me a boring, tasteless bottle of water. I couldn't help but notice the difference in demographics between the denizens of Deep Valley and those of Collins Beach. There was an arbitrary demarcation between the clothed beach and the nude one. Near this imaginary line sat an elderly, gray-haired couple, the color of mahogany, sharing fruit and bagels. Closer to the water sat three women in their late teens or earlier twenties. Two out of the three lacked tan lines. The third, jarringly pale in the chest and derriere, reclined prone as though trying to even up her tan lines. Their fourth compatriot, deeply tanned, frolicked in the fresh water for a bit before rejoining them on a large blanket.

We passed a group of Mexican men, presumably farm workers, huddled in the shadows. All of them wore dark jeans and T-shirts. Occasionally one of them would shuck his pants and wade into the shallow water in his boxer shorts. I remarked to Lisa that I found it odd that they didn't disrobe.

She shrugged and said, "Their culture is very modest, so they rarely go nude. I've always thought our society was a bit weird with regard to clothing, though. I could walk down the street in a bathing suit and nobody would think I was weird, assuming it was a warm day. But if I were to saunter down Main Street in my bra and panties, I'm sure some people would be concerned with my mental health. And what's the difference between undies and a bathing suit? Fabric? Isn't that weird?"

I agreed that it was. The same applied towards drug use, I thought and became lost in thought for a minute. Standing on your front lawn with a beer in your hand was normal, I reasoned. Wheeling by on a gurney with a needle in your arm was considered abnormal, pathological even. I needed to turn my brain off again.

Lisa plodded across the sand towards the volleyball court. "Want to play?"

"I'd love to." It had been years since I had played volleyball, but I was willing to give it a go.

Being a young, attractive woman, Lisa had no difficulty at all obtaining spots for us on the sandy volleyball court. Four bronzed, middle-aged men shuffled around their positions to accommodate us. Before long, we were leaping and spiking. Well, Lisa was, anyway. I was just doing my best not to embarrass myself.

Fully naked and demonstrating her considerable athletic prowess, Lisa was a pleasure to behold indeed. She spiked and dove, her taught muscles alternately relaxing and tensing, returning the serve with the power of youth and athleticism. Within a short period of time, my muscles acclimated and remembered the last time I had played volleyball in college. As I dove for the ball, my genitals, unencumbered by clothing, flopped about wildly, subject only to the forces of gravity and inertia.

Nobody kept score and at least half seemed to be a little inebriated, despite Collins Beach's official policy. Every once in a while, a participant wandered off to his towel to hydrate or to rest, only to be replaced by another. Finally, Lisa decided to take a break, so we bid our teammates adieu and took a dip in the cool, clean Columbia River. The silt under my bare feet was smooth and comfortable. I splashed, somersaulted, and floated on my back. It was absolutely glorious. Lisa waded out to where I was frolicking and embraced me. She smelled of Coors Light and sunscreen. We held each other and kissed.

"Lisa, the water suddenly just got warm," I said.

She giggled. "Sorry, babe. I've had a few beers." She kissed me on the lips and then flipped onto her back, floating. "Isn't this awesome?"

"That it is. I wouldn't want to spend it with anyone else but you."

When we got a bit chilled, we headed back and planted our asses on our blankets. Without suits, we dried off within a few minutes. My manhood took longer than that to come back to normal size.

We spent eight amazing hours at the beach, soaking in the sun. I realized when it was too late that I had taken on the complexion of a steamed lobster. In my enthusiasm to apply sunscreen to Lisa's back, I had forgotten to apply any to my own. As the sun began to go down, we packed up our gear. Reluctantly, I donned my shorts and found that the fabric on my burned skin was quite uncomfortable.

"Got a sunburn," I mentioned unnecessarily.

"Oh my God!" said Lisa. "You're as red as a beet! I've got some aloe I can put on you tonight. I'm sorry. I'm a terrible friend. I should have put sunscreen on your back. Why didn't you say something?"

Since Lisa had left all of her clothes in the truck, she had to walk naked into the parking lot, though it seemed she had planned it that way in keeping with her exhibitionist tendencies. When she did cover up, it was only grudgingly. She put on her T-shirt and wrapped a towel around her lower half. "You should probably drive," she said, and handed me the keys.

We arrived at our home away from home and immediately removed our clothing, as had become our custom. Lisa had forgotten to open a window or turn on the air in the trailer prior to our departure so at first it felt like we were being microwaved in a tin can while the air conditioning slowly reduced the interior temperature to a reasonable level. Dinner was a couple of sandwiches that we hadn't eaten at the beach, washed down with Gatorade.

"What time is it?" asked Lisa.

"About six."

"Shit. We forgot to call your parents. You should probably call and cancel. You feel like having another beach day tomorrow?"

"Sure. We can start out early and then call my parents and see if we can meet up in the early evening."

"Sounds good." After finishing her sandwich, Lisa cuddled up to me. "I can rub that aloe on you now," she said.

Aloe rubbing morphed into mutual full body rubbing, which inevitably progressed to sex. Having a sunburned willy wasn't a particularly comfortable experience, especially when it came to sex, but the endorphins released were a natural painkiller. We were asleep in each other's arms by eight p.m.

ROOSTER ROCK

My phone rang at 7 a.m. the next morning. I checked the caller ID. It was Grandma. "Hello?" I said groggily.

"Well, where the hell are you?"

"Oregon, Grandma."

"Doing what?"

My inner teenager considered responding "You mean doing whom?" but I thought better of it. Grandma had a robust sense of humor but I wasn't so sure if she would have been amused by my little joke. "Oh, just seeing a friend," I said. Lisa began to stir beside me.

"Seeing your dad and mom?"

"Might do that tonight."

"Well anyways, you haven't come to see me in days. Did you hear the news?"

"What news?"

"Well, Bob called me. I assumed he'd talked to you. Earl White was meeting with the realtor to sign final paperwork on selling the park. Apparently, somehow, he got the news that Dolores's will had been found and that she had left three million dollars to Deep Valley! I guess she left another million to ferret rescue or some damn thing."

196

"Ferret rescue? Well, that's a bit odd."

"Have you ever been to her home? Smelled like a public restroom. She had four of those little varmints. I think they must have escaped after she passed away."

"Never liked ferrets," I said. "They remind me of marginally polite weasels."

"I couldn't care less," said Grandma. "As long as they aren't Yorkshire Terrors!"

"So what is Earl planning to do with the three million dollars?"

"Well, he backed out of the deal with the preacher. He's using the money to rejuvenate Deep Valley! Looks like he won't be selling the park after all!"

I was floored. "That's great news, Grandma! I had no idea Dolores was so wealthy. I mean I knew she wasn't hurting for cash but…"

"None of us did. Earl says he'll put the money into improvements at the park, make it more attractive for the younger generation, you know? Hopefully we won't have to worry about money for a few more years at least."

"Awesome. And you'll get to keep your home and won't have to go live with a bunch of old farts."

"That's the hope," said Grandma. "Doctor says I might be discharged next week to home. I'll still need a walker for a while, but I'm going to get my strength back. Oh! And I quit smoking!"

"You'd mentioned that. For real this time?"

"Got me one of those nicotine patches. They taste terrible."

"Grandma, you've got to be kidding me."

"Oh yeah. I'm just pulling your leg. I've got to go. Nurse Ratched is here with my medicine."

197

Grandma hung up. Lisa was now sitting up, a cloud of blond hair obscuring her sleepy face. She rubbed her eyes. "What's up?" she said.

"Dolores willed most of her estate to Deep Valley, apparently, to the tune of three million dollars. Earl White backed out of the deal with the preacher and took Deep Valley off the market."

"Really? So we don't have to move?"

"That's what it sounds like. At least not for quite a while."

Lisa was out of bed now. If it were even possible, she looked even better with a deep tan. She swept her hair out of her face and tied it up with a rubber band. "We should celebrate. Want to go to breakfast? It's kind of our thing, isn't it?"

"Sounds great. Do you know of a place around here?'

"No, but we'll find one." Lisa hurried to the bathroom, peed and hastily brushed her teeth. I searched my bag for a suitable pair of shorts and a T-shirt with a minimum of wrinkles. By the time Lisa had finished her bathroom routine, I was seated by the door, waiting for her.

"Ready?" she asked.

"Yep."

Barefoot, with a spring in her step, Lisa descended the short set of stairs from the fifth wheel and nearly bounced out onto the gravel, keys in hand.

"Lisa!" I shouted. "Aren't you forgetting something?"

She looked genuinely confused. "No, what?"

"Clothes! You have to wear clothes!"

"Do I?" she said playfully. "Oh I guess you're right. Toss me a pair of shorts and a T-shirt. I have like four pairs of flip-flops in my truck."

I went in and got her some clothes. "Here," I said, tossing the clothes to her as she stood in all her glory beside her truck. A car slowly drove past our site, slowing even more when the driver saw Lisa. "Oh and Lisa?" I said. "I'm pretty sure this isn't a clothing-optional trailer park." Lisa took her sweet time putting on clothes.

We had to drive quite a ways to find a restaurant. There wasn't much to speak of on Sauvie Island so we ended up heading into Portland, at least forty minutes away, before we found a Denny's. I didn't mind the trip, though, and I was beginning to feel more and more relaxed in Lisa's company all the time. Conversation flowed effortlessly, ranging from our relief at Deep Valley's salvation to our time at the beach yesterday. My clothing, however, was nearly unbearable. My skin itched like crazy from the sunburn and I suspected this one was bad enough to peel in a few days.

Denny's was, predictably, quite loud, so Lisa and I concentrated on eating and drinking coffee instead of making conversation. We discussed where we were going to go that day and Lisa's plan was to check out another beach, known as Rooster Rock, located east of Portland on Highway 30. It was the first officially designated nude beach in the United States and Lisa had heard that it was quite vast and offered hiking opportunities.

After breakfast we picked up some snacks and supplies at a local grocery store and then stopped at Walmart to pick up a beach umbrella. Lisa was of the understanding that there was no shade at all at Rooster Rock, which was just fine for her, but not so good for me. I had no intention of sitting in the sun after my experience yesterday.

After paying the day's admission fees, Lisa parked in a lot overlooking the beach. A steep set of stairs led us to one of several sandy trails that took us down to the beach, clothing required on one side and nude on the other.

Predictably, upon descending the staircase, Lisa stripped off her clothes and threw them into her backpack. Physically she was only minimally lighter without her T-shirt, shorts, and shoes, but it was almost like I could see a metaphorical weight lift off her shoulders when she got naked. She looked like she hadn't a care in the world. The sun was noticeably warmer than it had been in Washington. The summer temperatures in Portland averaged about ten degrees higher than in the greater Seattle area.

In contrast to Lisa, I remained fully clothed and had even purchased a broad-brimmed sun hat that certainly won me no style points. I felt I looked like an old man, trudging along behind Lisa, towing our giant wheeled cooler, with my long-sleeved shirt and a hat that resembled an inverted flowerpot.

At the end of the trail, the beach became a massive, flat expanse of clean, wet, beige sand. A few people were scattered here and there, some basking on beach towels on the river side and others congregated on a swimming slough bordered on one side by brush and on the other side by a large chunk of land known as Sand Island. We had to walk quite a ways, wading through shallow water warmed by the sun, until we made it to Sand Island. There, we found a relatively flat spot and set down our towels. I got to work erecting my umbrella while Lisa strolled down to the shallow water of the Columbia River, skipping as she went. She was like a kid in a candy store.

I was parched after the long walk from the parking lot and slugged down some water while watching Lisa frolic about. If I had to stay in the shade today, at least my scenery was good. I dialed my parents' number into my cell phone, giggling a little to myself as I wondered what they would think if they knew where I was and what was in my field of vision. I imagine Dad would be proud of me. I apologized for having not got back to them the previous day. We arranged to meet at six p.m. that night at McMenamin's Restaurant in Portland.

Since I hadn't planned to frolic in the surf or tan my blistered hide, I brought a book with me and was perfectly content to read in the shade and cast frequent glances at my new girlfriend, who alternated between trying to see how far she could wade out into the water without going in over her shoulders and basking prone on her towel. As it turned out, Lisa could wade for quite a ways into the water, until she was a little speck in the distance and still was only in to her waist. It looked as though she could actually wade the Columbia River to the other side.

Eventually, even Lisa grew bored of her splashing and sunning routine. After much convincing, she managed to cajole me into taking a walk with her up the beach. I removed my shorts, but left my shirt on, unbuttoned and put on my silly hat. It was a ridiculous outfit, but it worked to keep the sun off my shoulders and head.

We held hands intermittently and walked the length of the beach, far away from the regular beachgoers. Soon our only companions were birds and an occasional annoying flying insect. We spotted a bald eagle perched on a piece of driftwood and were able to get pretty close to it before it flew off. For some foolish reason, I tried to climb one of Sand Island's massive dunes all the way to the top but it proved to be like quicksand. A third of the way there I lost my footing and tumbled. Lisa laughed at me. At least my landing was soft. I suspect that seeing naked people fall is easily twice is funny as seeing clothed people fall.

A motorboat full of reveling twenty-somethings zoomed by close to shore. The men whistled and hooted at Lisa. Apparently they had conveniently "forgotten" that it was a nude beach. Lisa just waved and blew them kisses as the rooster tail disappeared off into the distance.

Finally we reached a point at which our bare feet began to squish into thick, dark, smelly mud and we decided that was a good point to turn around. We had reached the tip of Sand Island and could see cars rushing by above on Highway 30.

"Do you think anyone can see us?" I asked.

"I hope so," replied Lisa, giggling. She had asked me to keep her phone in my shirt pocket and she took some silly pictures of us. I just wondered what she was planning to do with them. Social media for nudists?

On our way back, we spotted our friend the eagle again, having returned from a fishing expedition, an inert fish grasped in his talons. We passed a lone nude man making his way slowly up the beach with the aid of a stick. He smiled and waggled his stick as we passed each other. I decided that the atmosphere at Rooster Rock, at least on Sand Island, was decidedly different from that at Deep Valley. Whereas Deep Valley was about socializing and community, Rooster Rock was more about communing with nature—nudism and naturism, different but also complementary. And it was really nice not having to wear shoes for the entire walk.

Upon returning to our towel, I was pleased to see that nothing had been stolen, as we had just blissfully wandered off without a thought. Lisa laid back down, on her back this time, and evened out her tan. She took one last dip in the shallow water before we packed up and headed out. We still had to make it back to the trailer on Sauvie Island so we could shower and get ready for dinner. It had been a spectacular beach day, despite my sunburn.

After we had arrived back to Lisa's trailer, we made it a point to prove that two people could actually fit somewhat comfortably in an RV shower. We took turns lathering up each other's naked bodies, paying special attention to certain parts, but there wasn't time to finish our amorous activities before leaving to meet my parents. When I got out of the shower, I could have used my penis as a towel rack.

I put on a gray button-up shirt and a pair of slacks, then waited in the living area, playing Solitaire on my phone while Lisa shut herself in the bedroom for what seemed nearly a half an hour.

Finally, she emerged, wearing a blue dress and matching heels, her hair done up in a braid, wearing lipstick and mascara. The dress was just short enough to be sexy, but not so short as to seem risqué. It was an appropriate Meet the Parents outfit. She looked stunning and it occurred to me that I had never before seen her wearing make-up. In fact, I had never seen her dressed up before. Her daily attire usually consisted of shorts and a t-shirt or nothing at all.

"What?" she said, self-consciously. "Is this okay?"

"Okay? You look gorgeous."

Lisa did a little mock curtsey. "Why thank you, Dr. Bowman."

"I'd say I was undressing you with my eyes, but you know that doesn't make any sense," I said.

Lisa laughed and smacked my thigh playfully. "No it doesn't. Come on or we'll be late."

As we approached the entrance to McMenamin's, Lisa said, "I'm nervous about meeting your parents."

"Don't be," I said. "They're nice people."

"I'm sure they are, but you're still married."

"I thought of that. I'll just have to introduce you as my friend."

"Come on, Brian. They aren't stupid. Don't you think they'll be able to see through that?"

"Well, we'll just have to play it cool."

Lisa held my hand as we walked into the restaurant and let it go as soon as we walked through the door. My parents were already seated at a table by the window and arose to give us both hugs as we approached. I introduced Lisa and my parents greeted her warmly.

Of course there were the usual compulsory questions. "Where did you two meet? Lisa, what do you do for work?" Lisa was honest and said that we had met at Deep Valley and that she was a long-time member. As it turned out, her parents had met mine at a function years back when my parents had come to visit my grandmother, so they had a little bit of common ground.

Lisa deflected a bit when she was asked about her work and finally, after some mumbling, said that she was in the "environmental hygiene" business, which I thought was hilarious. Finally she admitted that she was a housekeeper.

"Oh, fantastic!" said my father. "Can you come clean my house?"

Lisa and I exchanged glances. Lisa said, "Certainly. I'll be sure to dress appropriately," at which point I vigorously bumped her knee under the table. Lisa startled. My dad looked somewhat bemused, took a sip of his whiskey and Coke, and changed the subject. Mom just sat there and smiled as she always did.

Lisa ordered a chef salad and a glass of wine, which I was afraid would hit her awfully hard considering how little food she had ordered. I ordered a burger and fries. After a while, conversation flowed easily between my parents and Lisa and I thought they were quite taken with her.

When it came time to pay, my father insisted on paying and we engaged in a tug-of-war for the bill. Dad won, triumphantly slapping down his card and scribbling his signature. It looked like he had left a pretty hefty tip as well. Our waitress was very pretty, and it was Dad's habit to tip well, especially if he had had something to drink.

We exchanged hugs in the parking lot and parted ways. I insisted on driving Lisa's truck back to the trailer as she was a little tipsy.

"Your parents are nice," she said.

"They are. I was afraid you were going to out yourself when my dad asked about what you did for a living."

Lisa laughed. "I know. I had fun with that."

We arrived back at Lisa's fifth wheel and immediately stripped off as had become our custom lately. We laid down on the bed on top of the covers, both too sleepy to engage in any other activity. Lisa's hands were folded neatly on her bare belly. She closed her eyes and sighed.

"Brian, what do you like about me?"

"Fishing for compliments, are we?"

"Just curious."

"Well, just look at you. What's not to like?"

"Be serious, Brian. I know what I look like. I mean, besides the fact that I'm blond and naked and lying right beside you."

"Well, Lisa, I love that you live your life without shame. You don't let anyone else tell you how to behave and you couldn't care less what other people think of you. Also, you're one of the kindest, most genuine people I've ever met."

Lisa smiled, her eyes closed. "Thank you, Brian. I know it seems like I'm fishing for compliments but I've never been a very confident person. People think because you're young and pretty by society's standards, you've got it made. Well, it isn't true. I so often feel I'm on the outside looking in. Guess I'm still trying to find where I fit in life. Does that make any sense?"

"It does."

Lisa closed her eyes for a minute and I had thought she had fallen asleep before she spoke once again. "You know what I'd really like to do?"

"Couldn't begin to imagine."

"I'd love to take a trip somewhere far away in a couple of months. Maybe Mexico. You ever been?"

"Never have."

"Me either. Want to go?"

"I might be able to swing it," I said, "for a week or so. Can't be too expensive, though. I don't think we could afford one of those all-inclusive places."

"Right," said Lisa. "And you probably couldn't be nude at those places anyway. I'm thinking a little bungalow on the beach or something."

"Sounds really nice. Let's plan it. Have any idea what you'd like to do tomorrow?"

"Not really. Probably not the beach. I'm kind of beached out."

"Let's go to Seaside on the coast. I used to go there as a kid with my family. I've got a lot of good memories from those days. What do you think?"

"Can we be naked?"

"No. I think we'd get arrested if we tried to walk the promenade naked."

Lisa thought for a second and then replied, "I guess you're right. It sounds fun. We don't always have to be naked to have fun."

At some point we drifted off to sleep together.

SEASIDE

We took off early the next morning for Seaside, Oregon, and arrived there in a little over two hours after stopping once for gas. Traffic was light, and Lisa had remembered to put on clothes this time—before leaving the trailer.

Our first stop was breakfast at the Pig 'N' Pancake, a locally famous establishment that had been serving customers since the early 1960s. Afterwards, we took a leisurely stroll on the promenade, holding hands and watching the kites dip and whirl as the ocean waves rolled in, enjoying the sun on our faces and the cool breeze that came in from the roaring surf. We window shopped for a bit, buying a little trinket here and there, and then stopped at an ice cream shop and enjoyed a cone while sitting outside on a bench, people-watching.

We had left Lisa's fifth wheel back on Sauvie Island with plans to pick it up in a couple of days when we had returned from Seaside, so we stayed in one of the few motels still left with a vacancy. Predictably, it didn't have an ocean view, but it was reasonably clean and inexpensive. After spending the afternoon seeing the sights of Seaside, we came back to the motel for a long late afternoon nap followed by a casual dinner of Chinese take-out.

The next day we started our day out again at the Pig 'N' Pancake and then spent the morning at the aquarium, taking our time to go through all the exhibits and learn all about the various marine creatures. I offered my unsolicited expertise at certain points, but Lisa didn't seem to mind. Afterwards, we walked the beach itself, felt the mist from the saltwater on our face and listened to the roaring and crashing of the waves. Next we decided to check out the nearby town of Cannon Beach and took a long beach walk there. All was serene and peaceful, but much colder and windier than the two Columbia River nude beaches we had visited. For the two days that Lisa had to wear clothes, she didn't complain a bit and actually seemed to really enjoy herself.

When we checked out of the motel the following morning, I felt a little sad as our road trip was coming to an end. We headed back to Sauvie Island to pick up the fifth wheel, but not to frolic on the beach this time. We had had such a great time and I was really not looking forward to the reality of work and bill-paying that awaited us after the very long trip home to Skagit County.

AND SUMMER TURNS TO FALL

Come August, the days became noticeably shorter and then in mid-September, the rains predictably returned. Tents were taken down and trailers were hitched up and moved out for either storage or the refuge of warmer climates in the south. Only a handful of full-timers remained, most of them hunkered down for the fall and winter months with a supply of good movies and plenty of coffee.

Lisa continued her daily naked runs for as long as possible into the fall and I joined her when the mood hit me. As September turned to October, Lisa added a baseball cap and T-shirt, remaining naked from the waist down on her runs, but finally it became too cold for her as well and she gave it up until springtime. She took to exercising indoors in front of the television, naked of course, with five-pound weights and resistance bands. I always enjoyed watching her as I took up space on her couch, eating chips and drinking those tasteless seltzers. On occasion I would even join her but found myself to be fantastically uncoordinated for any kind of yoga movements. Lisa laughed at me, good-naturedly but often.

At first it made me depressed to see the rains come, but my indoor time with Lisa became a source of growth for our relationship. Whereas in the summer we would hike and swim and occasionally run, in the fall and winter we found ourselves playing a multitude of board games and cuddling up to watch movies in the evenings. We had coffee with each other most mornings, either at my place or hers and both of us kept the temperatures at our respective trailers at seventy-five degrees so we could be comfortably naked all winter long.

Grandma had returned home one day, triumphantly, minus the walker, plopped herself on her old couch, and flicked on the television. Not much had changed except for the lack of cigarettes. I had picked her up from Mira Vista nursing home one morning. When I arrived to retrieve her, she was already sitting in the hallway, dressed and ready, with a small suitcase beside her. Her return to the presidency was an easy transition, as it was the off-season and she had little to do. I had no qualms about turning over my office to her. After all, I hadn't done much to begin with other than attending a few meetings and helping out around the club a little more than I would have before. I guess in a way, though, I had a hand in saving Deep Valley, after having uncovered Dale Parkhurst's sordid history, so I felt good about that.

Grandma didn't mind having Lisa around as long as she and I confined our romantic interludes to Lisa's trailer. During the days when I worked at the university, Lisa would often come over, drink coffee, play cards, and keep company with Grandma. A nudist club could feel pretty quiet and lonely when the sun wasn't out.

Lisa's nude housecleaning service began to rise in popularity in the fall, perhaps it was because the many single men who used her services spent many a lonely day by themselves in the darkness, staring out at the rain. When I was available, I tagged along with her as she served her many clients, under the auspices of being a chaperone. The large, wall-eyed man she had spoken to me about weeks earlier was every bit as odd and creepy as she had described him, though he seemed more lonely than dangerous. He had simply sat at his kitchen table, wheezing slightly, stirring his drink, while Lisa, clad in fishnets and heels, sanitized his already immaculate house. Lisa always asked for money up front, in cash. At one point, she calculated that she had made $3,000 from that client alone in crisp, fat bills, but to gaze around at his mansion and his small fleet of luxury cars, it was nothing but a drop in the bucket to him.

My divorce with Jennifer was final at the end of October, which was certainly a relief and about as equitable as could be, considering the circumstances. I was just thankful that we didn't have a house to sell or children involved. Paying a good chunk of change every month to my ex-wife was a real ball-buster, but it was a small price to pay for getting my life back on track. For the first time in a very long time, I was beginning to see glimmers of hope in my future.

TROPICAL VACATION

Lisa and I finally made it to Mexico in November, which for me was one of the most depressing times of year in the Pacific Northwest. It was too early for snow, at least a month away from Christmas, and the prospect of not seeing the sun for five months loomed large. It was great to be back in the sun again, if even for a few days.

We stayed in a bungalow just a few yards from the beach, down a narrow but steep trail. The stretch of beach in front was mostly deserted, so we could use it nude, though it wasn't officially designated as such. Every once in a while, a tourist would wander past and we were usually able to spot them in the distance early enough to cover up with our towels as they strode past. Lisa did fall asleep one day on the beach while I was taking a nap inside and a local boy passing through got an eyeful. She only awoke because he had dropped his bottle of Corona on a rock in surprise. Lisa being Lisa simply lifted her head up from her towel and waved. When she told me the story later after a Margarita or three, she couldn't stop laughing. Every day, I was beginning to appreciate more and more her unabashed approach to her body, to life in general. In fact, I was beginning to feel I loved her and I sensed that it was mutual.

Though the palapa provided some shade from the sun, it was still nearly eighty degrees Fahrenheit underneath where I had set up my chair and table. A slight breeze provided welcome relief, wafting hints of sargassum. I certainly wasn't complaining after the winter we'd been experiencing in the northern hemisphere. An iguana basked outside on a rock, pausing briefly to bob its head in acknowledgement of a passing neighbor. I briefly wondered if the chirps of the tropical birds in the palm trees above could be picked up by my laptop's microphone.

Lisa and I had spent the previous two days soaking up all the luxuries Mexico's Riviera Maya had to offer, well, those that could be enjoyed nude anyways.

I took a sip of my coffee, strong, bitter, and conspicuously absent of my habitual Baileys. I had to keep a clear head if I were not only to teach but to answer questions from my inquisitive new students. My button-up shirt was draped over an adjacent chair, awaiting the appointed time at which I would transform from carefree nudist into online professor of biology.

As I waited until my Apple watch alarm went off, just five minutes before 0800 Pacific Standard Time, I wandered into the casita. Lisa was up already, frying bacon and cutting up mangos and pineapple for breakfast. Her long blond hair, absent her usual braid and unkempt from a night of sleep, cascaded over her shoulders and down her back, hanging nearly to her bare buttocks. I pushed a lock of hair behind her right ear, gently kissed her cheek, and ran my hand from the small of her back to her buttocks.

"Easy, there, Professor," she said with a slight smile. "You have to be molding young minds in a couple of minutes."

"Yeah, yeah, yeah." As blood flow increased to my own south of the border, I was grateful that the camera would only capture me from the chest up.

Butterflies danced in my stomach. Maybe it was the result of too much coffee, or perhaps it was the thought that I was back in my element, teaching. Only this time, it was on my terms and from the comfort of a beach chair.

I smoothed the towel that I had previously set up on my chair and settled in, wearing nothing but a pair of worn flip-flops and the sunburn of one not accustomed to the intensity of the sun on the Riviera Maya. I removed my Oakleys from the top of my head, brushed my hair a little bit, and then donned my button-up shirt. After smoothing my shirt out, I put on my glasses, round, wire-rimmed, professorial, I thought. I opened up my laptop and focused the camera on my face. I was naked from the waist down and nobody would be the wiser.

"Welcome to Biology 348, Anatomy and Physiology for Health Care Professions. I'm your instructor, Dr. Brian Bowman. This semester we'll be exploring in depth the various organ systems in the human body, the maintenance of homeostasis, and most importantly, the body's capacity to adapt to challenging circumstances and its capacity for healing."

As I flipped through the Power Point presentation, an introduction to the course, I felt the same thrill I had experienced before when I had just started teaching. The information flowed out of me like a river, and I felt once again that I was where I needed to be, the way I hadn't felt in a very long time. I was making a positive difference, not only in the education of students, but in my own life.

215

After fifty minutes, I bid the class goodbye until the next day and concluded the session. I closed the laptop and looked up to see Lisa standing in front of me naked with one bare foot up on chair. The way she held her towel just in front of her pubic region, her eyes slightly downcast, made her seem at once demure and playful.

I took a final sip of my now lukewarm coffee and arose from my chair, leaving the towel behind. Lisa dropped her towel on a nearby chair and turned to face the casita, then skipped merrily inside with me in pursuit.

Whatever should I do with the rest of the day?

EPILOGUE

The following year, on June 1, a bright, sunny day without a cloud in sight, there was a small ceremony at the park to honor Dolores and her posthumous contributions to the park. Cake and coffee were served in the newly renovated clubhouse, adjacent the pool/hot-tub area with its many upgrades.

Lisa and I sat in the back, clad in our birthday suits. Over the winter, we'd gotten engaged and Lisa sported a modest but sparkly diamond ring on her finger. Mr. Dan, proprietor of Bare Spirits and all-around nudist dinosaur, had given his blessing of the union, despite admitting disappointment that he himself couldn't marry her. Lisa had found an online paramedic program based in Boston that allowed her do all of her didactics remotely and her clinical time locally. Though it was challenging, she was enjoying her schooling and she was excelling. The woman was smart as a whip. My career was finally rebounding. I split my time between video lecturing and teaching lab full-time at Skagit Valley College. It was a good fit. And I had been sober for nearly a year.

All of us in the clubhouse were naked with the exception of Grandma, who wore the longest T-shirt on Earth and a pair of worn bedroom slippers. She had quit smoking for good and had recovered nicely from both her fractured hip and her stroke. All that remained was some weakness in the right hand and some almost imperceptibly slurred speech. She had put on a few healthy pounds that filled out the wrinkles and she actually looked years younger. She had also started walking, very slowly, around the park every morning, a habit she had kept up since being released from the hospital. "I want to live to see ninety," she had said. "Or at least until I meet my first great-grandchild." She had given me a knowing wink. We were working on it.

In the last year, the park had attracted some younger members, a true feat in the age of dwindling nudist club membership nationwide. The volleyball court had been restored and there were usually a few games played every sunny summer weekend. Even some of the oldsters took to the court and some lost a few pounds in the process. A large, flat, unused area of park property had been turned into a mini-golf course and I came to realize that I'm even worse at nude golf than I am at clothed golf. Even if it didn't bring in any new members by itself, the mini-golf course served as one more entertainment venue to keep new members busy and interested.

The crowning glory of the newly restored Deep Valley Family Nudist Park, though, was the Dolores Eisenberg Memorial Water Park, a monstrous creation that stood one-hundred feet tall and boasted two waterslides, one of which snaked a lazy path to the wading pool below. Adjacent to it was The Drop, a waterslide that was set at a terrifying sixty-degree angle. Even though I had only worked up the courage to take that ride once, I found it to be an exhilarating experience, even if I was the recipient of an unwanted water enema out of the deal. Oh, the perils of nude recreation!

Now when Reverend Dale Parkhurst stands at his picture window attempting to enjoy his morning coffee, he can scowl down at the naked people getting ready to ride the waterslides. Sometimes they wave at him, knowing he's up there, displeased and muttering to himself. He doesn't wave back. Only one person I know of has ever flipped him the bird. I won't say her name, but it starts with L.

In the end, Grandma got to keep her house, and that was what I had worried about most when the park was in peril. Lisa and I moved into a new park model at Deep Valley with a great view of Lake Haussmann. Grandma knows that if she needs anything, we are close by and Lisa and I are committed to keeping her in her home and caring for her until the very end. There was simply no way I would let her go to a nursing home.

In an ultimate irony, it came to light sometime after Dolores's death that her husband had made his fortune as a CEO in a textile business. I often wondered what the late Sam Eisenberg would think if he knew that the money he made selling maternity clothing ultimately saved a nudist resort.

I'd like to think he'd be pleased or, at the very least, mildly amused.

About the Author

Matthew Franklin Sias was born in soggy, gray Seattle, Washington, and has inexplicably lived in the greater Seattle area ever since. He is a member of the American Association for Nude Recreation and generally avoids getting dressed whenever possible, though his employer appreciates it when he remembers to wear pants to work.

In his spare time, Gary paddles his kayak on the frigid Puget Sound, wanders about on the beach and looks at tide pools, gardens au naturel (much to the chagrin of several former neighbors), runs (clothed of course), dabbles in the practice of emergency medicine until he gets it right, and attempts to raise two little girls, of whom he is very fond.

This is Matthew's first fictional novel, and the events and characters therein are loosely based on his experiences as well as mishaps in the eclectic world of nude recreation.

Always remember your towel!